CW01498536

CONTENTS

FOREWORD TO THE 2009 EDITION

The question 'A science of God?' was raised by Austin Farrer (1904–68) in the mid twentieth century. He used it as the title for a book of Lenten sermons that was published at the invitation of the Bishop of London in 1966. At the same time, this very book, *A Science of God?*, was also published in the USA but was even more provocatively titled *God is not Dead*. Ostensibly, Farrer's intention was to counter the philosophies of atheists such as Friedrich Nietszche (1844–1900) and Jean-Paul Sartre (1905–80).

Whether God is alive or dead, in an increasingly scientific and technologically advanced world, questions related to the origin of the universe and the origin of life remain perplexing. Even now, in the twenty-first century, eminent scientists such as Paul Davies, with no particular theological axe to grind, continue to wrestle with these enigmas. In his recent publication, *The Goldilocks Enigma*, he suggests that inadequate attempts in science and religion to explain the origin of the universe may rest in their methods of approach. Further, in the future with advancing scientific enquiry, all may be swept away and replaced by revelations as yet undreamt of, which will explain why things are as they are (*The Goldilocks Enigma*, Allen Lane, 2006, pp. 292–3).

By contrast, Christof Koch, in collaboration with Francis Crick, has commended that, despite 'philosophical and religious proclivities', it is better to concentrate research on what he calls the material correlates of consciousness in the brain and their properties (*The Quest for Consciousness*,

A SCIENCE OF GOD?

by

AUSTIN FARRER

Originally published in Great Britain in 1966 by Geoffrey Bles,
52 Doughty Street, London WC1

This edition published in Great Britain in 2009

Society for Promoting Christian Knowledge
36 Causton Street
London SW1P 4ST

British Library Cataloguing-in-Publication Data
A catalogue record for this book is available from the British Library

ISBN 978–0–281–06150–1

1 3 5 7 9 10 8 6 4 2

Printed in Great Britain by Ashford Colour Press

Produced on paper from sustainable forests

Roberts & Co., 2004, p. 303). In this way, scientific method can forge helpful inroads into the study of consciousness, achieve great advances in learning through neurobiological research and escape the dilemmas posed by higher order questions.

For those with a scientific background and an interest in religion, however, the problem cannot be dispensed with so easily. Whether one is engaged with the study of cosmology, evolution or the big bang, the problem of creation still remains unresolved. Even scientists without an interest in religion are left with a need to provide an adequate explanation for the *origin of the universe* from a secular world-view. If chance or necessity is not the answer, how is one to account for the origins of life and our world? Can divine action be discerned? Is some new scientific methodological approach required as Paul Davies has suggested, or are higher order questions best evaded?

The poignancy of Austin Farrer's question 'A science of God?' holds increased significance in a contemporary world. For instance, even Alister McGrath, who has produced a mammoth three-volume work entitled *A Scientific Theology* (subtitled *Nature, Reality* and *Theory* respectively) and explained the insights of his trilogy succinctly to a wider audience in his small book entitled *The Science of God* (T&T Clark, 2004), acknowledges how this massive undertaking revealed to him the manifold difficulties involved in expounding a scientific theology. In his concluding remarks to his trilogy he says: 'The process of unfolding what seemed like a bright idea back in 1978 has proved to be far more difficult than I had imagined, and its execution less satisfactory than I had hoped . . . What I had hoped might be extensive discussions of central methodological questions have ended up being rather shallow . . .' (*A Scientific Theology*, T&T Clark, 2002, Vol. 3, p. 295).

The question persists: is a science of God ultimately possible? Put more precisely, to what extent is a serious, scientific and critical approach to theology achievable?

Writing well ahead of his time, Farrer's thought would now appear to have even greater importance. In 1966, while others were engaged with more conventional approaches to theological enquiry, Farrer was credited with being an original, independent and unique thinker. In contemporary terminology, he could be described as a person well skilled in 'thinking outside the box'. Thus, in his book *A Science of God?*, he says that his main intention is to exhibit 'the sort of parallel to scientific activity which religion offers. That is, I am taking religion as an exploration of realities, the realities in this case being divine.' His reason is simple: '. . . once we have called the truth of religion in question, we begin to grope for the realities it purports to describe, and until we feel we have encountered solid fact, cannot well get on with the practice of our faith' (p. 112).

In *A Science of God?*, we find Farrer adopting an approach that is both fascinating and critical. In Chapter 1, with wit and delightful humour, he dismantles wrong-headed approaches to theology and the sciences. His discussion in Chapter 2, 'God and the Stars', makes clear his recognition that, in scientific exploration, wonders about the origin of life and the universe inevitably arise. However, he also notes that if one is to search for an understanding of divine will, a study of astronomy alone cannot achieve an answer to such questions.

Instead, the creation of life is what needs to be addressed. Thus, in Chapters 3 and 4 he presents his argument for the creation of life. At the time of his writing in the 1960s, perplexing conflicts between theology and the sciences over biological evolution and creation were proving as problematic as their continued prevalence in our current world.

Interestingly, the full import of Farrer's question, 'A science of God?', is demonstrated in Chapter 5, 'The God of Nature'. His discussion of the perplexities confronting theologians and scientists alike with respect to the origins of life and the universe is profound and illuminating. He adopts a methodology that can be shown to be *'more scientific'* than present-day arguments used by evolutionary biologists, such as Richard Dawkins, to counter 'creationism'. At the same time, he makes clear to theologians the principles of enquiry that have to be observed critically in defence of divine creation if one is to avoid a host of impending pitfalls.

Farrer argues: 'We must approach the evidence in a scientific spirit, and examine all available evidences in a scientific way; not only the evidence *for* but equally the evidence *against*' (p. 10). Further, he holds that the scientist has every right to demand of theologians that claims to knowledge of God be open to scientific investigation: 'the facts, whatever they are, need careful sifting . . . We shall have first to ask what they actually suggest to us, or what is the best account we can give of them' (pp. 11–12).

His recognition of the necessity of a multi-disciplinary approach to acquire an understanding of ourselves and our world, in which the contribution of critical theology is rightly included, makes obvious the importance of the re-publication and re-reading of his book. His thought is amazingly pertinent for contemporary times. In addition, Farrer's skilful and investigative reflection on science and theology helps bring to light unexpected insights. It will be by reading his plain prose descriptions of evolutionary theory, the creation of life and experimental proof that one is most likely to be convinced of encountering *genius*.

Margaret M. Yee,
St Cross College, Oxford

FOREWORD TO THE 1966 EDITION

In an age of much doubt and confusion there are few remedies so helpful as books that insist upon the concrete, positive, affirmative elements in the Christian faith. Our Lent Book this year will be found definitely among that small and select number. In particular it should enable us to meet the argument that, because of the discoveries associated with the theory of evolution, God has somehow been swept off the stage of world affairs into the wings, where he has no longer any part to play in the great drama of life.

✠   Robert Londin:

I

THEOLOGY AND SCIENCE

The series in which this book appears might reasonably lead its readers to expect something directly concerned with holy living. But even among people well disposed towards religion there is at present much uncertainty and much confusion of mind about the mere belief in God. And so I have thought it most useful to write about that fundamental issue. Those who do not want to discuss it with me can read something else. For those who wish to nourish their souls on edification, I can, however, offer the hope of a few crumbs; for we can scarcely establish the grounds of belief without making the belief itself more vivid, relevant and clear.

I mean to talk about the matter, and the matter alone, and to invite my readers to think with me, that they may make up their own minds. I do not propose to report the views of enthusiastic theologians with foreign names; for that sort of thing, though no doubt stimulating, is of little use for the settling of our convictions. I propose to approach the being of God, and to approach it calmly, treating it as a matter of knowledge. We will not talk about faith, or anyhow not to begin with. Anyone can see that faith is the attitude appropriate towards the God of Christians. Supposing we believe that there is such a God, and supposing we are reasonable beings, we shall trust him

to do for us what the Gospel promises in his name; and trusting is faith. We shall trust him, if he exists, but we can hardly
trust him to exist. We must have reason to think he does.

Whether anything of a particular kind exists, appears to
be a scientific question. Not, of course, if it is obvious that
the sort of thing is there. We do not call in scientific pro-
cedures to shew that there are dogs and cats. To illustrate
the point we should need a more out-of-the-way example.
For instance, is there such a thing as second-sight? Well,
evidently no such *thing*, if you want to be pedantic. Second-
sight isn't a thing – not an organ, like an eye, nor an instrument, like a receiving-set, which some Highlanders or
Gipsies are lucky enough to possess. It is alleged to be a
sort of mental "seeing" which these people can achieve.
But can they? That is the question; and it is a question
which is only to be answered by a very careful sifting of
evidence. It is not good enough, to let ourselves be convinced by the tales people tell us. We must approach the
question in a scientific spirit, and examine all available evidence in a scientific way; not only the evidence *for*, but
equally the evidence *against*.

Science goes further, though. It is not very scientific to
let people fix on you a question like "Is there such a human
power as the exercise of second-sight?" "Wait a bit," says
the scientist. "What sets your inquiry in motion? Popular
belief in the supposed fact. Very well; popular belief is not
to be despised. Unless there were some odd-looking experiences happening here and there, I dare say the popular
tales would never have circulated. But the scientific question is not, 'Are the tales true?' It is 'What would be the
most accurate account we can give of the facts which in-

spired the tales?' Let's be generous; let's suppose that the human mind, or the Highland mind, really is capable of knowing things through channels other than those which common sense recognizes. A scientist may still not want to say 'So you see there is second-sight'. It may be quite misleading to bunch all such out-of-the-way knowings together, and to label them with that name. We shall want to see what is the best way to describe and to classify the facts our inquiry uncovers."

The scientific thinker might expect it to be the same with our (alleged) knowledge of God. God's being, like second-sight, is a matter of common belief. It seems to call for scientific investigation, for if it is a fact it is not an obvious fact. Adam in the old story meets God walking in the garden, just as Eve a little earlier has met the snake crawling there. But that is poetry, and it would be very dull-witted of us to take it literally. If we are going to talk poetry, let us come a few thousand years nearer to our own times. "They reckon ill who leave me out" says the voice of God in a famous line of American verse. The line may be poetry, but it's the sort of poetry which puts prose in a nutshell. For believers in God do quite soberly claim that an account of things which omits his presence or his action is incomplete: "They reckon ill who leave him out." And it would be surprising for the claim to be so widely and so confidently advanced as we see it to be, if there were no facts anywhere even seeming to demand a theistic interpretation. Very well; but the facts, whatever they are, need careful sifting; and when we have sifted them, it will not be scientific to use them without more ado as evidence for or against traditional religious belief. We shall have first to ask what they actually suggest to us, or what is the best account we can give of them.

Most people have taken a hand some time or other in a debating-society. The procedure is stereotyped. At any given meeting a motion is on the table, and anyone who speaks is bound to speak to the motion, whether for or against. If he talks at large round the subject, the chairman will call him to order. It's the rule of the game; a game, however, which has more to do with politics than it has to do with science. It is not congenial to the scientific mind to debate set proposals; to be obliged (for example) either to support or to oppose the motion "that this House believes in the God of Abraham, Isaac and Jacob". The scientist's inquiry would be more like this – What are the facts which suggest religious ideas to people? And what is the explanation, or the description, which these facts call for? Religious belief as such will have its importance for the pure scientist, on the principle that there's no smoke without fire. He may think, that is, that facts of some kind have most probably given rise to the belief, and that the facts are worth looking into. What we cannot fairly expect of him is that he should accept traditional religious statements as though they were the products of scientific thinking, offered as scientific hypotheses are offered, in explanation of the facts. We cannot present him with the Creed, and say, "Here's your hypothesis; get down to work and test it on the data." For he is free to protest, "But it isn't my hypothesis; and I shall not know whether to take it as mine, until I have had a good look at the data for myself."

What I am trying to do is to state a scientific attitude to religious belief. I am trying to present it fairly, and unbe-

devilled with small-minded prejudice. By "scientific attitude" I do not mean "dogmatic materialism", although I
know that is what it stands for in many people's minds.
The scientist they think of is a physical scientist, and they
imagine his principle to be this: "Physical fact is my business; and what isn't my business doesn't exist." There can
be found physical scientists who behave as though they
thought so, but that it is not because they are scientists; it's
because they are men. It is a very human failing to say
"What isn't my business is nobody's business" – very
human, very understandable; but scarcely respectable for
all that.

The small-minded scientist says: "I've got a wonderfully
accurate and useful method of inquiry into nature, and an
enlightened government has given me and my colleagues a
few million pounds' worth of equipment to employ on the
job. What can't be handled by our methods and with our
tools may as well be written off." The large-minded
scientist says, "We've had great good luck with the
physical sciences in the last couple of centuries. The results
show that we've got to grips with natural fact in a uniquely
effective way. Whatever scientific work may or may not
have taught us, it has shown us what it is like to be up
against facts, and how facts have to be respected. Neither
our methods nor our tools will tackle every sort of fact,
but the general attitude to fact which we have developed
should go with us, into whatever fields of inquiry we move,
and whatever methods or tools we take up."

Our small-minded scientist's attitude is an absurdity, if
not a caricature. No one with a drop of decency in his composition would sign his name to the statement we have just

attributed to the man. If people fall into such postures, it is through human weakness. They do not go about saying, "That's my philosophy." The large-minded scientist's attitude is, on the contrary, an honest taking-to-heart of the lesson which scientific discovery has taught the world. It is called "Empiricism".

Having reached this point, we can attach some definite meaning to the suggestion that we ought to have a science about God, or (what comes to the same thing) an empirical approach to theology. It is the suggestion that there are some facts on which religious belief rests; that these facts can, and should, be looked at with an impartial eye, and by the best or most accurate means available to us; and that having made our observations, we should not use them as ammunition either in support or in defeat of existing doctrines, but rather set old theories aside while we consider what description or explanation the observed facts genuinely call for. So we shall construct our theory with all due caution; and having constructed it, test it on the facts and see whether they square with it.

No decent thinker who has grown up in the scientific tradition can help feeling sooner or later that the empirical method ought to be tried in theology. Not that the attempt is certain to succeed; only that the scientifically trained Christian will have no peace of mind until it has been made. Perhaps we shall manage to do some empirical theology; or perhaps, in attempting it, we shall discover that theology cannot be fully empirical, and why it cannot. In either case we may hope to satisfy our minds.

If we are to have a science of God our requirements will be these:

1. Some solid and relevant facts
2. An effective and reliable method of studying them
3. The ability to form appropriate theories
4. A method of testing our theories on the facts.

The first two requirements will be enough to start with; the facts and the method of observing them. And before we ask, "Which facts?" we had better ask, "What range of facts?" For we are using the model of natural science to guide us in our religious inquiry; and the first thing that may strike us about scientific investigation is that it may be concerned either with an unlimited range of facts, or with a limited range. We can inquire (for example) in the limited range whether there really is anything like a new manlike species, the so-called Yeti, in the Indian mountains, or a dragon-like reptile in the waters of Loch Ness, or a small planet, invisible to common observation, somewhere beyond Neptune or Uranus; and go on to inquire (if our conjecture proves well-founded) just what the zoological character of the animal, or the mass and composition of the planet, must be. For an investigation into an unlimited range of facts we cannot pick a better example than the whole inquiry into the basic nature and action of that physical energy which we take to be the stuff of all things. The inquiry is not concerned with a limited group of physical facts, but with all physical facts whatever and wherever they may be.

Which sort of inquiry shall we take for our pattern in theology, the limited or the unlimited? We might be tempted to take the limited, on the ground that the facts or situations are few, in which people are inclined to say that the action of God strikes them with anything like the force of evidence. But on the other side there are terrible and notorious difficulties besetting the limited approach. If we say that a limited range of facts alone concerns the being or action of God, we treat him as a factor among the factors which go to make up the universe. Such was, and is, the belief of unreflective pagans. They take the universe to be made up of various active beings – inanimate forces or bodies, plants, beasts, men, and gods few or many. That is paganism; and paganism will not do. The story of its breakdown is familiar. The pagan gods, being parts of the world, come under the survey of natural science; they are found to be unobservable as realities and unnecessary as explanations. The thunder isn't Jove or Thor banging about; it's an electric explosion. And electric explosions in the clouds need no god to touch them off; when electric charges pile up in the clouds and clouds with opposite or unequal charges are within range, the explosion follows as a matter of course. So the gods get elbowed out by the inferior agents with whom they were supposed to share the world. Inanimate forces, plants, animals, men are found to do all that gets done. There is nothing left for the gods to cause, and so no evidence that there are any.

You may think that we make it too easy for ourselves by taking the example of thunder. Who does not know that Jupiter is dead? When people think of a limited range of facts as showing the hand of God, they mean spiritual facts. No one any longer believes in a god of lightning; people are still inclined to believe in a god of enlightenment. God does not blast us, he inspires us; if we are going to talk paganism, he is Apollo, not Jupiter. Very well; but if Jupiter is dead, Apollo is dying. Jupiter was exploded by meteorology; Apollo is eroded by psychology. We know more, certainly, about the weather than we know about the mind – more about thunderstorms than about brainstorms. Yet it would be a foolish theologian who claimed of any "inspired" thought or feeling in a human heart, that it could be the work neither of nature nor of man, but of God alone.

The remark I have just made is liable to be misunderstood. I am not denying that the reality and the action of God come through to us particularly in moments of inspiration. It would be suicide for any believer in God to deny that. What I am denying is that godhead can be conceived of as a limited agency with its own little range of effects. The action of God must be taken to be universal. But when we claim this, we cannot be expected to claim that God's active presence comes home to us with equal clarity at every point in the universe. There is more theology to be dug out of a saint than out of a sandpit.

The admission is perfectly harmless; it does not even put our theology out of line with our physics. A physical law may have the widest conceivable scope, and cover every movement of energy (let us say) in any corner of space. But not all cases of its exemplification are equally telling, either in first bringing it to the notice of science, or in helping students to see the force of it once it has been established. Einstein's doctrine about the curvature of light has universal application; it was forced upon his attention by a comparatively narrow range of highly specialized observations. The accepted account of the forces tied within the atom covers every particle of stuff anywhere to be found; yet to amateurs (though I dare say not to professional physicists) one atomic explosion gives more evidence of the doctrine than any number of encounters with high winds or brick walls. Believers will read God's action into everything; they will not pretend that it everywhere equally strikes them. Great tracts of experience may seem flat and godless; the light breaks on us in occasional bursts of godhead.

In fact it is not the width of what we have called the unlimited range of scientific investigation, that puts a difference between its field and the field of theological inquiry: it is the shallowness of it. The range of a scientific exploration may be boundless; the depth cannot be. Wherever there is a surface of water, the hovercraft can go; it cannot plumb the deeps of ocean. In drawing the comparison I am not talking mysticism, or making conventional claims for the "depth" of religious thought, whatever such claims might mean. I am stating a simple fact about all sciences: they are selective. Not necessarily selective in picking out one thing for attention and turning a blind eye to another thing. A science such as physics may cover everything in the world; but it does so by selecting one aspect for consideration, and turning a blind eye to any other aspect there may be to anything.

"Look out!" a kind friend at my elbow says to me, "or you'll find that you've given away your case. A theologian can't afford to admit that any physical science covers everything in the universe, even if it's only on its physical side. Some things have no physical side. In your view, there are physical realities and there are spiritual realities; and the spiritual realities aren't physical." Grateful as I am for my friends' well-meant warning, I propose to brush it off.

There *is* a physical side to everything in this universe. Are there pure spirits, with nothing physical about them? I very much hope there are; but I am sure that they aren't in the universe. How could they be? The universe is a physical system, and nothing that is not physical can hold a place in it. I am in the universe, for I am sitting in this chair; and nature has kindly provided me with a sitting part. Am I nothing but body, then? Is not my mind real? Real? Yes, certainly, but not separately so. There is a fly, now, crawling across my paper. The little wiry legs are real, and so is their action in crawling; if the legs weren't real, the fly could not crawl with them; and if the crawling were not real, the legs would be at rest. The crawling isn't the legs, neither are the legs the crawling. Yet the crawling is not separate from the legs; and no more are the surprising activities of imagination and thought separate from the bodily person, so long as this life endures. Christians trust God to give them another life apart from flesh and blood; they do not suppose it will qualify them for retaining a lodgement in this physical universe.

"But you think that God is pure spirit; and surely you think he is in the universe." Ah, but how? We will come to that in due course. It will be enough to say here that God cannot possibly be placed in the universe as one of its constituents is placed; like me, for example, sitting in my chair. The highest spiritual achievements attainable *within this world* are still the activities of bodily creatures; and so there is nothing in the world which, on some side of it, the science of physics does not touch.

On some side of it – not on the whole of its bodily side. No one with the least smattering of scientific learning will suppose that the field of physics is drawn narrow enough by being simply equated with the bodily. There are many aspects of bodily existence which the science of physics discounts. Physics is concerned with forces active upon forces, in so far as their action is measurable. At the beginning of the modern scientific movement, round about the later sixteen hundreds, philosophers were tying themselves in knots to justify the scientist's rigid selection of measurable facts from among the whole rich mass of man's bodily experience. We can afford now to laugh at those philosophers. Their agonies of thought might have been spared. Nothing needed to be justified, nothing called for any explanation. Why shouldn't certain scientists study the measurable action of forces on forces? If they were going to study that, then that's what they would attend to, and any attention paid to other aspects of things would be merely distracting. No one expects a geometer to attend to anything but flat areas; so why should a physicist attend to anything but forces mutually engaged?

The selectiveness of science, so far from being an oddity, is the very lifeblood of the method. If you try to deal with all aspects of anything at once, your inquiry gets completely choked with your data. Progress begins to be possible when you pick a question sufficiently particular to be decided, and an aspect of things sufficiently specialized to be investigated. No one attempts to trawl by scooping up the ocean in watertight buckets; one must use a mesh wide enough to let go what one does not want, and to retain what one does – the marketable fish. It would be conceivable (though certainly not remunerative) for trawlers to drag the whole ocean-bed. Still they would bring up nothing but sizeable fishes, or other bodies of comparable bulk. It is conceivable that physicists should rake the whole universe of bodily existence. They would still collect nothing but measurable actions of force on force. That is what their instruments register; that is what their method handles.

Perhaps more than enough has been said to recall the well-known truth that a science needs not only a range of facts to go upon, but a sieve for selecting its facts. Physics covers everything in the universe; but only in a certain aspect. Now what about our theological inquiry? It seems tempting at first sight to draw a close parallel. Theology, too, claims to touch upon everything in the universe; but only in a certain aspect of it. Physics deals with the force-relation between everything and everything else; theology deals with the dependence-relation which ties everything to God.

The parallel sounds good, and it is good – so far as it goes. But there remains one enormous difference. Physics has a sieve for fact; theology has none. By the time a physicist has told himself what his science is about, the sieve is in his hands. He is looking for energies acting measurably on other energies. So there's his sieve; that's what he'll collect; everything else he will let go. He knows what sort of facts concern him, and what do not. The theologian has no such luck. Suppose he says to himself, "I will look at the God-related aspect of things, and let all other aspects alone." How is he to do it? Which are the "God-related aspects of things"? Or rather, which are *not*? How can a theologian possibly say that anything, or any aspect of things, is by its very nature unrelated to God? Must not

everything be related to him if anything is? Admittedly
not everything, nor every aspect of things, strike us as God-
related; but that does not mean that we can write off whole
realms of fact before we look at them, as having no light
to throw on the religious quest. For one never knows where
the God-relatedness of things may not come out. One man
will tell you that the mechanical sequence of cause and
effect, the soulless regularity of the physical order, is of all
things least revealing. Yet it is a simple fact of history that
many minds have seen the touch of God supremely manifested in the rational order of the physical world. The
sentiment finds expression in hymns which, even now, we
sing with every sign of hearty participation, praising the
sovereign Legislator who

> has spoken;
> Worlds his mighty voice obeyed;
> Laws which never shall be broken
> For their guidance he hath made.

If, then, theology is a science, it differs from every other
in having no sieve for the relevant fact. As a celebrated
rhyme declares, "Geography is about maps; biography is
about chaps." And theology? About God, obviously; that's
easily said. But it does not tell us what in the world to look
for. Personal facts and mappable facts are no trouble to pick
out, whereas it seems that God-manifesting facts cannot be
picked out at all; or anyhow, not on any scientific principle.

But that's not the worst of it. It is not merely that
theology is unprovided with a sieve; it is that she firmly
turns her back on the whole business of sieving and attempts the very opposite approach. The scientist limits his

attention to a carefully skinned-off aspect of things, to their physical, chemical or biological characteristics. The religious thinker does his best to get rid of all one-sidedness and to see things in depth and in the round. And naturally; for what is to indicate God to us, if it is not the things that actually exist? Natural laws are of concern to science; but they don't *exist*, on any showing. There exists a vast number of active beings or forces, which agree in functioning on principles which our so-called "laws of nature" attempt to describe. Neither chemical nor biological structure exists; there exists a host of substances or of creatures structured in certain standard ways which chemistry and biology define. If we are to approach God through the things whose existence manifests his activity, our attention will be held by the real beings to which the diagrams of scientific thought apply, and not by the diagrams.

Religious people have sometimes drawn the careless conclusion, that because science works by selection and theology by rounding out, theology has no concern with science and can ignore it. They have been content to base their religious thinking on a pre-scientific, commonsense reaction to the world, helped out, maybe, by poetry, mythology and art – by whatever charm or skill, indeed, can help us get the "feel" of things. This is a very short-sighted policy. If the religious approach is concerned with the whole picture, it is concerned with everything that can contribute either detail or order to the picture. The map of the countryside is not the countryside, but if you are trying to get the countryside into your head, the map will help you. It is a pity to think of nothing but the map, and miss the country; but it is a pity also not to organize your vision of the country by the help of the map. Musical theory may distract one from the enjoyment of music. It need not – on the contrary, those who know the theory can greatly enhance their perceptiveness for musical quality by a scientific appreciation of musical structure.

No doubt it is all too possible for students of scientific cosmology to substitute bloodless world-diagrams for a contemplation of the living universe. But the bias can be corrected; and then how enormously the mental picture of the universe is enriched by the astronomer's diagrams! Take all scientific doctrines away, and you can scarcely be said to have any picture of the universe at all. What indeed would be left you, beyond the ideas suggested to an ignorant child by the sky on a clear night? A blue expanse, powdered with points of fire, all, no doubt, a number of miles away from you. No adult capable of reading a book conceives the universe after such a fashion. We all of us conceive what scientific observation and scientific theory have taught us to conceive. What, then, is the difference between our knowledge (such as it is) of scientific theories and our full-blooded thought of the universe? – Only the difference between a consideration of the patterns or rules, and a recollection of the numberless real physical beings which make up the patterns or go by the rules; when we reflect that at every point in the enormous system there is a live event, held in place and conditioned by the whole field of other events, and drawing into the focus of its momentary occurrence rays from a circumference wide beyond imagination and bafflingly complex.

The part played by scientific notions in our full-blooded thought of things varies greatly in different provinces of our knowledge. In our thinking about the universe, science provides the whole skeleton of our idea, apart from which it collapses into nothing. For contrast, take our thinking about the animal creation. In this realm common sense, and our immediate understanding of our fellow-creatures, will give us a considerable body of knowledge sound in itself, and capable of standing up on its own. Science nevertheless enriches the picture with much fascinating detail, say about the minute structures which carry the functioning of animal life. And if we are to be stirred by religious amazement at that marvellous thing, a living animal, the intricacy of the structure and the delicacy of its physical controls will contribute to excite our wonder.

It is nonsense, then, to say that because a science separates out its chosen aspect from things, while a religious approach heaps all the aspects of a thing together, the religious approach has therefore no use for the scientific fact. On the contrary; the aspects which a religious approach heaps together will include aspects on which science has cast a brilliant and an unforgettable light. It is, in fact, absurd for a modern man to suppose that he can clear his mind of scientific ideas, whatever he may be thinking about. We are bound to think in the way our age and civilization have learnt to think. Our science may be slipshod and out of date, but still it will be science; and its being slipshod and out of date will make it no better for theological purposes.

2

GOD AND THE STARS

We have said that the person who wants to find his way into theology should look at the real beings which compose the world; and that he should look with all his eyes, with all the understanding that science or any other serious and reliable method of thought can contribute. He must not make up pretty fancies, or tell himself old-world tales; he must grasp realities as fully and as surely as he is able.

Well, but if we stare at the world, or at the creatures that compose it, we may stare till we are blue in the face, and see – What shall we see? The world, or its component creatures; we shall never see God. Joseph Addison, in his somewhat wordy paraphrase of Psalm xix, says about the stars:

> What though in solemn silence all
> Move round the dark terrestrial ball?
> What though nor real voice nor sound
> Amid their radiant orbs be found?
> In reason's ear they all rejoice
> And utter forth a glorious voice
> For ever singing as they shine
> "The hand that made us is divine".

The stars, says the poet, do not actually shout "God made us"; the declaration of God's glory which the Psalmist had attributed to them sounds "in reason's ear". And reason's ear, we may think, is a somewhat mysterious organ. It is no use feeling for it under your chin or behind the back of your head. To open "reason's ear" upon the matter can only mean to approach it with the right apparatus of ideas for the job. The skilled detective has an ear for the evidence, or an eye for the clue, not because he hears or sees any better than the rest of us, but because he has got the problem set up in his head, and so the newly observed fact drops straight into a mental slot prepared for it. The detective (anyhow, the novelist's detective) may well say that the fact cries aloud, or speaks for itself.

> What though no real voice around
> The fishy circumstance resound?
> In reason's ear . . .

If Addison, or if the detective claims to pick up the overtones of meaning with *reason's* ear, he does not only mean that his mind is stocked with relevant ideas, he means that they are the right ideas and that they bring out the true significance of the fact. If a prejudiced judge and a fair-minded jury are sitting together in court, hearing the pleas of learned counsel, then the judge, for all his superior apparatus of legal ideas, is not listening with reasons's ear; he is listening with the ear of prejudice. Reason's ear, if it is in the court at all, will be found attached to the juryman's head, in spite of his lack of legal background, and comparative simplicity of mind. Had Addison been willing to shut reason's ear, and listen to the message of the stars with the ear of poetical fancy, there was a flood of old-world notions ready to fill his mind and make him "hear" the starry heavens, as they swung round, sing like concentric humming-tops, one within another, each giving a distinct note, the whole set making up an octave – the so-called "harmony of the spheres". But one of the things his poem expresses is his sober refusal to "listen" thus.

> What though in solemn silence all
> Move round the dark terrestrial ball?

There is no "music of the spheres". Yet "in reason's ear they all rejoice . . ."

Addison, as a serious thinker, is convinced that it is with reason's ear he listens; he brings to bear a system of ideas which he takes to be valid, and such as to elicit the truth from the fact. And if we are to make the world, or anything it contains, speak to us of God, we shall need to do likewise.

It is the stars that speak – no supernatural voice cuts in to tell the poet the message of the skies. If nature is to speak to us of God, the reasonable "ear" we turn to her must be a set of ideas which so clarify the character or the structure of natural fact itself, as to show its dependence on a Higher Cause. What set of ideas will do this for us? We have seen how large a part scientific ideas play in giving shape to our picture of the universe. Are not they just the ideas needed to throw a bridge back from the creation to its Creator? The answer, as usual, is not simple. We must insist that however important a share science may have in making our evidence speak to us, the actual movement of our mind in going from the world to God is always a jump beyond science. And so, if anyone asks whether belief in God is "scientific", we are bound to answer Yes, and No. Yes, for it can be the following out of thoughts started by science; No, for it cannot be a piece of science itself.

There is nothing suspicious about a guarded answer of this kind, as a familiar example may show. No one can call a publicity-campaign against excessive smoking a piece of scientific activity. It is not a piece of science, it's a piece of publicity. But scientific researches into the effects of heavy smoking may provide the whole impetus behind the campaign; and they may also be said rationally to justify it. In a broad sense you might call the campaign "scientific" though not in the narrow sense. Anyhow, nobody who accepted the soundness of the research behind it would want to call it "unscientific". We reserve that ugly name for beliefs which sound science would lead us to discard, or for activities it would lead us to break off.

The reason why the movement of the mind from a view of the world to a conviction of God cannot be a piece of science can be stated quite simply. It is because of what science is. Every science picks out an aspect of things in the world and shows how it goes. Everything that lies outside such a field lies outside the scope of that science. And since God is not a part of the world, still less an aspect of it, nothing that is said about God, however truly, can be a statement belonging to any science.

For example, astronomy and physics are about the distributions and interactions of forces, including masses of conjoined forces composing what we call bodies. A sentence, if it is to find a place in physical or astronomical science, must state either a rule about the way forces act, or a particular fact (known or suggested) about the way some force or mass of forces has acted or will act. Since God is not a rule built into the action of forces, nor is he a block of force himself, no sentence about God can play a part in physics or astronomy.

There is a hackneyed anecdote about Napoleon. The Emperor asked Laplace, the astronomer, where the action of God came into his calculations. "Sire," he replied, "we have no need of that hypothesis." We may forgive Laplace – he was answering an amateur according to his ignorance, not to say a fool according to his folly. Considered as a serious observation, his remark could scarcely have been more misleading. Laplace and his colleagues had not learnt to do without theology; they had merely learnt to mind their own business. Astronomy goes from physical fact to physical fact for ever, by the light of physical rules. It may have to guess at explanations, but these explanations will be states of physical fact not directly observable, or rules of physical action suggested but not yet sufficiently tested. How could God come into the astronomical story?

"We have no need of that hypothesis." Was Laplace claiming to have found an astronomical explanation for the whole distribution of matter in the observable heavens? If he was, his boast was utterly unjustified. There was plenty of unexplained fact in Laplace's picture of the world and if anyone liked to find an explanation for it in the will of a Creator, Laplace could not say that the explanation was uncalled for; all he could say was, it wasn't astronomy. As an astronomer, he could pass no judgement upon it; as a man, he might condescend to have a try. Parallels are easy to quote. A mathematician cannot, as a mathematician, calculate the probable happiness of a marriage; he can only work out such things as the financial profit or loss to the parties. But that does not mean that no mathematician can make a sensible marriage. It only means that mathematicians, as well as being mathematicians, are men.

We have dropped into talking about astronomy; and indeed it seems the obvious field for nature-theology to take. We suppose that the mind moves from the world to God; and the astronomer is the man who takes the world – that is, the universe – for his province. Certainly astronomy, in its cosmological department, is unrivalled for raising ultimate questions; but that need not mean it is the best area in which to look for an answer.

Astronomy raises ultimate questions; of course it does. Whenever we look for the explanation of any single thing or any single happening, our inclination will be to look for it somewhere in the world. We shall hope to find a previous state of affairs leading naturally to what we are trying to account for; or to find forces already in position and capable of having produced it. For practical purposes we shall commonly be content to push the inquiry no further. But if we are looking for ultimate reasons, we shall need to explain the facts which have served as our explanation; and so on, step by step, back and back for ever. All explanations carry us backwards up the stream of some history or other; and all lesser histories find their place and origin in the vast history of the universe.

Explain me, if you like, as the product of human history. Very well; but human history comes out of the history of man's animal ancestors, and theirs by development from the first living organisms on the earth's surface. So we come back to the history of the earth's crust, and how it came to be in such a condition that life could arise upon it. We shall have next to ask how the earth came to have a crust; and behind that, how the earth came to be, as a solar planet. So back to the origin of the solar system itself, and then of the galaxy in which it finds a place; and of galaxies in general. So the ultimate questions fall into the lap of cosmological astronomy; and behind astronomy we cannot go; not, that is, on the scientific plane.

Astronomers carry the history of the universe back as far as they can guess. They can never reach an absolute beginning. It is an instinct of the human mind to prefer the simple explanation to the complex; and following that instinct, some scientists have suggested that our whole unimaginably vast universe began from one tremendous explosion, out of which matter scattered, and has continued ever since to scatter over an ever widening area. It may well be that some such story best explains how the matter of the universe we know comes to be distributed as we find it to be. It gets us no nearer a beginning of things, for there is no more reason why physical reality should have originally consisted in one great head of concentrated force, than in a widely-scattered system. We shall still have to explain why the explosion happened when it did, and what was the state of things before the explosion. If there was nothing to explode, then nothing exploded; and if nothing exploded, there was no explosion. "But isn't it a neat theory, that one all-powerful God created one universe, by simply creating one all-powerful explosion?" Perhaps it is; but whatever it is, it isn't physics; it's a jump beyond science, for it's a jump beyond the world.

Cosmological theories have a short life nowadays and the "great primeval burst" may be on its way out. In any case it is being emphasized that the burst is not a beginning. The development which we trace from it is not *the* development of *the* universe; there may have been, and for all we know may yet be, any number of such developments, one after another.

Whether we think the universe had a beginning in time, or think it has always been going on, we come up against a brick wall, so far as explanation goes. We can hope to explain any state of the universe, or any detail in it, from the previous history of the universe, and from the way the world runs. But if we ask why it has the sort of history it has, or runs as it runs, there is no answer within the scope of science.

"And no answer outside it, either" the atheist thinker rejoins. Explanations hang upon facts. You cannot offer an explanation unless you have some facts on which to base it. Sheer unexplained facts are bound to come first in any explanatory story. Asking for an explanation to stand behind all facts is just silliness. If we do it, it is simply that we have got into the habit of asking the question "Why?" and go on asking it, after it had ceased to mean anything. An endless quest for explanation has been praised as a divine discontent. In fact it is a propensity most characteristic of rudimentary minds. "Why does that man wear that hat?" – "Because he's a policeman." – "Why is he a policeman?" – "Because he wanted to be, when he grew up." – "Why did he want to be?" – "Because he wanted to earn his living." – "Why did he want to earn his living?" – "So as to be able to live; everyone does." – "Why does everyone want to live?" – "Stop saying 'Why?' darling, and go to sleep."

Yes. Some time we must stop saying "Why?" because we have reached the fact which it is senseless to question; for example, it is useless to ask why living beings want to live. But the issue between the atheist and the believer is

c

not whether it makes sense to question ultimate fact. The issue is, what fact is ultimate. The atheist's ultimate fact is the world; the theist's ultimate fact is God. If we could see no further than the world, the world would have to be our ultimate fact. But we think we can see further.

"So you think. But suppose you can – what good does it do you? You have still an ultimate fact to swallow; and what difference does it make pushing the ultimate fact one step farther back? You will have to swallow the being of God without explanation, so why not swallow the being of the world, with an equal absence of explanation? The atheist's position has at least the advantage of simplicity: it does without God."

No, you are wrong. The being of God does not have to be "swallowed". "Swallow" in this connexion is an offensive term. The figure of speech is drawn from the experience of gulping what will with difficulty go down; and it is applied to such unfortunates as the man who has always prized himself on his abilities and must reconcile himself to the fact that he is incapable of a university degree. If a fact takes swallowing, it is of the kind called indigestible. Now an unexplained world is indigestible; an unexplained God is not. An unexplained world is indigestible, because there is so much in it that cries out for explanation. Why should it be the way it is? Without ceasing to be a physical world, it could just as well have been quite otherwise than we find it. There is no ultimate reason for matter to have got into the curiously irregular systems of the galaxies – had astronomical history been different from the beginning, matter would now be differently arranged; and in that case I should not be sitting at this table pushing this pen, nor per-

haps would there have been any animal in the world with
the wit or the inclination to discuss cosmology.

So if the atheist says about an unexplained world "You've
just got to swallow it," he may or may not be right, but anyhow one can see what he means. If the world must indeed
remain unexplained, it takes some swallowing. Not so the
being of God. No one can be puzzled to see why God
should be the way he is. For the very meaning of the name
is a free, untrammelled Spirit, who is all that he sees it best
to be. The explanation of what he is lies in himself. To look
for an explanation behind or above or outside him is senseless.

"Senseless, perhaps, to ask why he is the way he is. We
could still ask why he is there at all." – Could we? I do not
think we could, except by parroting the word "Why?"
after it had ceased to mean anything; like the child we had
to silence just now by telling him to go to sleep. Have not
we agreed already that nothing but realities can serve as explanations? The basic reality, then, will be the basic explanation; and to ask for an explanation of its existence will
be senseless. For where could we look for it? Only in a
reality more basic and more self-explanatory. But "God"
means the most basic, most self-explanatory of beings there
are. If we found a good reason for supposing that the Maker
of the universe was not the basic reality, should we not
deny to him the name of God? Should we not say that the
universe had been created under God by an archangel of
some sort? The opinion has been held. There is little to be
said for it and I do not suppose anyone wants to hear it
discussed.

We said some little while ago that astronomical cosmology raises ultimate questions, but does not much help

towards answering them. It raises the question whether we ought to swallow an unexplained universe as sheer fact, or go back to a self-explanatory God. We have been showing that the supposition of God is not senseless or unhelpful; but that is not to say that the supposition ought to be made. Have we a right to demand that the basic fact behind which explanation cannot go should be a fact that takes no swallowing? The passion for neat schemes and tidy pictures is common to us all, and very naturally so. We want to get the world into our heads; we have a prejudice in favour of any account of it which will fit it nicely into our mental pigeon holes. So it would be a comfort to think of the universe as a single great process explained by a single personal Cause, himself self-explanatory. A pretty tale indeed, but why should it be true? Not surely because it is pretty. Ought not we to remind ourselves that facts are awkward customers and that reality refuses again and again to fit our neat little diagrams? Ought we not to see the task of the human mind as an unending struggle with a vast intractable fact, the universe, which our thought can never reach behind, through, around, or over?

"Well, but then how are we to suppose that the universe got started?" – There is no scientific evidence that it ever needed to get started – that it ever was not going. There are some indications that the part we know of it has worked into lumps, like a sauce under the hands of an unskilful cook – that clouds of more or less uniform gas have clotted into groups of stars. There are other indications, less reliable perhaps, that the stuff of the universe known to us has greatly spread or scattered over space. So we have reason to think that things were not what they are and that what is

now complex was simpler once. We have no scientific indications of a day when it all began. Indeed it would almost
qualify an astronomer for a mental hospital for him to
imagine that any reasoning he might base on present
observations could be trusted to follow a trail thousands and
thousands of million years back to a supposed origin of things,
and not get lost on the way. Poor little hypothesis, liable to
be wrecked on a myriad hidden reefs of old facts to us invisible, strewing the upper reaches of the river of time! To
try such a hypothesis would be like launching a rocket, not
at another planet in our own system, nor yet at the sun, but
at a star on the other side of the galaxy; hoping that it might
thread its way in safety between a few thousand thousand
stars, to reach its destined target; a target it could not anyhow hit until ages after those who launched it were dead.

Astronomy raises our wonder about origins; it does
nothing to satisfy it. Our thought flies into the outside of
space and into the backside of time. In both directions it
peters out, and reaches no end. It is impossible to believe
that, however far back we might go, we would find the
world any more self-explanatory than it is today. We
should still have sheer brute facts to swallow. We should
still be asking why the world was like that, rather than
otherwise; still asking without knowing how to decide,
whether or no the course things had taken had been chosen
and ordained for them by a sovereign will.

But if we are left in uncertainty by astronomical speculation we have no need to feel discouraged. On the contrary, we can draw a straightforward and serviceable moral
from our disappointment. The idea of finding God by
going back to the beginning, is mistaken. Since we shall

never reach a beginning we shall never make contact with the action of God by that route. If God's power is to be detected in anything which science can help us to see, it will not be in the way things started, it will be in the way things go. And the worst area in which to study the way things go is in the remote past of astronomical time, or in the far reaches of astronomical space. For we cannot hope to draw anything but the sketchiest outlines of regions so far remote from us.

Consider a parallel case. Suppose we wished to examine the evidence for a divine guidance of human history. Should we think it good sense to take for our field the lives of our remotest ancestors, about whom we know only what we infer from their bones? Obviously not. We should turn to the records of men who can speak to us. And so if we are to look for God's hand in the way nature goes, we shall take examples which can be more closely studied than the furthest margins of astronomical conjecture.

Our conclusion agrees with the principle we laid down for our own guidance in the previous chapter. The proper approach to a knowledge of God (we said) must be through the most full-blooded appreciation of our fellow-beings that we can achieve. The attempt to make our picture of remote astronomical matters full-blooded can never advance far. We can do little more than remind ourselves that the outline sketch our science provides is coloured in by the vigorous existence and lively interaction of innumerable energies. We can scarcely hope for such an insight into their being as might disclose to us anything in particular about their relation to a divine will.

3

THE CREATION OF LIFE (I)

The Bible-story of Creation records an activity of God
exercised upon a welter of stuff already there before he gets
to work upon it. That at least is a very possible way of interpreting the narrative. It takes us back to a beginning, but
what beginning? Not, on this view, any beginning of
physical existence, only the beginning of our stellar system.
So God would be described not as the creator of matter,
but only as the shaper of bodies.

Such a limited view of the divine action would have re-
ceived very general support in the ancient world. It was the
prevalent opinion among pious and thoughtful Greeks, by
the time Greek and Jew got to know one another's minds.
It is the more remarkable, therefore, that the Jews and after
them the Christians should have felt that the Bible was
against the Greeks; that Genesis really taught God's creation of the world out of nothing. The creative acts described there in detail and assigned to the first six days of
the week were not the first creative acts of God. A God
of such sovereign power must be supposed to have
supplied his own materials for his own handiwork. The
first words of the Bible should therefore be taken to
mean: "In the beginning God created heaven and earth;
and so there came to be an earth all anyhow, with dark-
ness on the face of the abyss. Then the breath of God

fluttered the face of the water and God said, Let there be light."

It might seem that when Jewish and Christian Bible-readers wanted to lay their fingers on examples of God's creative action, they found themselves directed towards his shaping of man's familiar environment, and of living things. At the same time in considering such examples, they were brought face to face with a creative power so absolute, that nothing could be left outside its scope; not even the first matter and primary stuff of the world.

I have quoted a page from the ancient history of ideas to show that there is nothing either odd or new in our own predicament. We are not the first generation to be baffled by the mystery of physical origins and to have nothing very clear or definite to say about God's action there. We are not the first to look rather at the shaping or development of creatures for the signs of a power sovereign over all things. And perhaps we, like our predecessors, may see reason to carry back God's creativity from the areas we can survey into that dark abyss of the dead and hidden past, which no glint of our exploring lamp can penetrate.

We want to think for ourselves about the theology of nature, and I do not wish to anticipate our conclusions by quoting our predecessors. All the same it would be a strange thing if the modern man's best reasons for believing in a Creator turned out to have no point of contact with the reasons which moved his ancestors in faith. They had no knowledge of basic physics and their astronomy was elementary. They fastened their eyes on the beautiful structure and the appropriate functioning of plants, animals and other visible parts of nature, and saw in these things the art of a creative wisdom. If we are to say that they were simply mistaken in their reading of the evidence, we can scarcely claim to inherit their belief. On the other hand we cannot look with their eyes. We cannot neglect the enormous enlightenment which scientific research has brought us. Our ancestors were looking at the same realities as we; they were not seeing them so clearly or so exactly.

"But if we do look as clearly and as exactly as we can, will any of the nature-theology remain? What about Charles Darwin? What about biological evolution? Have not the biologists handed in the same report as the astronomers – *We have no need of the theistic hypothesis*? Have not the intricate structure, the successful functioning of living things been revealed as the products of a natural process, working over an immense tract of time?"

Ah, but these are just the questions that we have to consider. Biology has followed the footsteps of astronomy, and has grown up in the last century or so. The biologists, like the astronomers, have learnt to mind their own business. They have realized that no statement about God can find a place in a book of biology, because biology is an account of biological species and of the way they go on; and God is neither a biological species, nor is he the name of a biological law, nor is he a factor in the environment of living things. No "God-hypothesis", then, can come into biology. It may still be, however, that living things and their histories, viewed with all the help biology can give us, will push us to jump on beyond science into theology.

As everyone knows, it is possible to wrangle with Darwin's disciples over the question whether the evolution of species in general has been proved, or merely postulated.

The actual evidence we have in the form of animal remains showing evolutionary development is very limited; and what it shows is rather development within a species than development of one species out of another. There is some evidence that man was once a more apelike creature than now, with a less degenerate jaw and a less elaborate brain. There is no direct evidence that I am aware of for the branching of men, gorillas and orang-outangs from a single stem. We cannot find traces of a time when the ancestors of the three species interbred as one kind.

Here is a cooling consideration, certainly, for hot-headed theorists. It reminds us that scientific generalizations should be advanced with becoming caution. Nevertheless it is really silly to dispute general evolution. On such evidence as we have, it is a supremely reasonable supposition. On astronomical and geological grounds we have to suppose that the conditions for the existence of biological species developed gradually, after the earth's surface settled and cooled; and it is difficult not to suppose that the species themselves developed gradually, too; especially as the means of life for any one species are largely constituted by other species. Plants feed on a soil enriched by vegetable deposit, animals feed on plants or on other animals. Elementary forms of life must be in position before the more advanced forms can flourish; and these again provide a nourishment for forms more developed still. That the forms of life must have come in gradually, is a conclusion one can scarcely resist.

The only alternative to an evolutionary account would be the supposition that new species were pushed in ready made when the time was ripe for them. This would be to make the Creative Power like the sort of gardener who keeps his grounds gay with bedding varieties ready grown, and planted out in full flower according as the season allows. From the scientific point of view, every introduction of a new species would be a separate miracle, defying scientific explanation; and it is impossible for any scientist to prefer such a view, so long as the evolutionary view is open to him. It is no use telling him that general evolution isn't proved; you will have to show him that it is impossible, before he will be ready to look at the miraculous alternative.

To sum up: the evolution of biological species is part of a total picture of the natural world, and it is not worth kicking at it unless we can have back the whole pre-nineteenth-century world-view. We might do happily without evolution if we could believe the solar system to be an ageless, unchanging mechanism, a perfectly constructed watch guaranteed never to run down until the Day of Judgement; if we could believe all the races of creatures to have lived side by side from the beginning just as they are, except that one or two species had been so unlucky as to die out through the combined force of disastrous accident. Since we are about as likely to believe these things as we are to believe that the earth is flat, we may as well stop pretending to make evolution an open question.

There is no need at this time of day to go over the lamentable tale of our great grandfathers' stupidity, when they resisted evolutionary doctrine as a threat to religious orthodoxy. It has happened again and again in the history of religion, that people have become so firmly accustomed to some one scientific setting for their credal beliefs, as to mistake it for part of the Creed. They cling to it when it has ceased to be scientific, and shrink from the mental agony of rethinking their position. However painful, the rethinking has now been done. The fury of the old debate has died, leaving us free to consider in a reasonable spirit the relation of evolutionary ideas to belief in God.

If we look at the matter broadly, there is one point which sticks out a mile. On the pre-evolutionary view, Creation (if you believed in it) was tucked away completely out of sight behind the beginning of the world. On the evolutionary view, Creation (if, once again, we believe in it) will be going on under our eyes in the production of new species. Well, not exactly under our eyes; but anyhow in a tract of time which we can look back upon and to some extent reconstruct from surviving evidence. Which view, then, the evolutionary or the pre-evolutionary, promises us the more direct confrontation with a creative God? The answer is obvious: the advantage lies with the evolutionary view. It must be more revealing to see the Creator at work, than to infer that he once acted before the world was.

To drive home the point, it will be worth recalling how uncertain a ground people had for believing in creation at all when the world was supposed to be a changeless system, with all the races of creatures as we know then fixed in their natures. Why should not such a world contain a built-in principle of self-maintenance? And if it did contain such a principle, why should it not always have been there, and have needed no creating? So Aristotle had thought, and Aristotle had been the most solid thinker of the Classical Age – perhaps, indeed, of any age; always allowing for the fact that he lacked some of our advantages. The best of the

Christian philosophers who afterwards borrowed his ideas admitted that they could not prove him wrong. We should not know, they said, whether the world had ever had a beginning, had not God inspired Moses to tell us. The modern believer is entitled to take a stronger position. If the highest forms of life can be seen to have developed from elementary systems of physical energy, the case for a creative pull of some kind, drawing nature upwards, is a case that cannot be lightly dismissed, Moses or no Moses.

One advantage, certainly, the pre-evolutionary theologians possessed; but it was an advantage which no honest mind can envy them. Since they placed creation at so safe a distance, tucked away, as we have said, behind the beginning of the world, they were free to imagine it according to their own sweet will. We, looking for it in the process of the knowable world, are obliged to square any picture we may draw of it with facts as we find them. Perhaps it was just this that hurt pious minds so much a century ago, when evolutionary ideas were first taught. It was not that Creation was being taken away from them, but that it was being pushed under their noses, and they could not recognise it; so different is fact from fancy.

And what is the difference? To take fancy first – if people are free to imagine creation, how do they imagine it? They think of God as being like themselves, only perfectly powerful. He is the perfect craftsman, the perfect engineer, exercising a perfect control over perfectly-chosen materials – indeed, so marvellous a workman is he, that he can call the materials into existence specially for the job in hand; and his control is so absolute, that he need engage in no physical struggle with the thing he is constructing. He wills it to be as he wants it, and so it is. The Creation of the world was the one perfectly clean job.

So we imagined, while we were still free to imagine. And what did Darwin and his disciples show us? A process of trial and error, infinitely wasteful and almost unbelievably slow; an undisciplined tendency of things to throw sports and chance-variations, checked by a merciless competition eliminating the less competitive; until at long last a creature appears with the physical ability to make tools and the vocal ability to make sentences. He breaks through into free thought, he replaces a natural by a designed environment; and there is man.

It was scarcely surprising if people who had imagined creation on the super-craftsman pattern failed to recognise what Darwin showed them as amounting to creation at all. But what's in a word? The question is not, whether our language-habits incline us to call the evolutionary process "creation". The question is, whether that process discloses to us the action of a divine power. We shall only confuse the issue if we first decide what we think a divine power might be expected to do, and then turn to the facts for a check on our theory. We ought to start with the facts, and simply ask whether evolutionary development can be accepted as a natural process which works itself out, or whether it is necessary to suppose a creative leading. If we decide for the leading, it will be time enough to ask the further question, what form that leading appears to take.

"Can evolutionary development be a natural process which works itself?" Such is the question we have thrown out. If we are to do any good with it, we cannot be content with so scandalously careless a formulation. *What* might or might not be judged capable of working itself? "The process of evolutionary development." But what on earth is that? Not a thing, nor yet a body of things. It is the outline description of a history covering millions of years and running through millions of generations. For comparison let us take something from the history of our civilization. It would not at all surprise us to hear the following remark. "The development of physical science, once set on the right lines by Galileo and Newton, continues to run on by its own impetus." I should call that a thoroughly sensible remark. But I should not take it to mean that there is a mysterious being, called Physical Science, which once set going, keeps charging along like a railway-truck. I should take it to mean something more like this. There is a certain amount of intellectual acumen and of inventive genius scattered up and down the human race – not much, indeed, but still a certain amount; and we have no reason to fear that it will dry up and disappear entirely. The scientific work of the schools deriving from Galileo and Newton keeps opening up questions for experimental inquiry, and it would be surprising if our clever men did not rush into the indicated areas and seize upon such tempting opportunities; especially since the practical advantages promised to mankind by scientific advance offer abundant motives, additional to the motive of intellectual curiosity. To make the story complete, I should add that physical nature is at once so regular and so complex, as to offer a virtually inexhaustible field for scientific exploration. So on all accounts the exploration is not likely to stop.

The story I have spun out is wordy and wearisome. It is to avoid such tediousness that we prefer imaginative remarks

like the saying with which we started: "Once set on
the right lines, scientific development runs on by its own
impetus." But the long-winded explanation has its merit;
it makes it clear that the inevitability of scientific advance is
grounded in the aptitudes, the motives and the situations of
individual men. And (to turn at long last from parable to
application) if we do wish to say that the evolutionary development of biological species is a process that works
itself, we shall have to say that the natures, the active
tendencies and the situations of innumerable creatures over
millions of years have been such as to bring it about.

Here am I, sitting in this chair and pushing this pen. The
thoughts I am writing down are certainly not original, but
neither are they altogether elementary. They range to and
fro over time and space, over fact and possibility, in a way
which would be highly surprising to a primitive man,
could he understand it (which of course he couldn't). How
did I get here and how did I get like this? The question can
be asked with even more point about those abler minds
who read these reflections of mine and pull them to pieces.
Each of us can trace the origins of his existence a few generations back. In view of the fertile marriages of four pairs of
great grandparents, and certain specifiable conditions since
obtaining, there was no particular difficulty about any one
of us arriving on the scene. But now take the inquiry a little
farther back – a negligible period, no doubt, in the total
history of the universe – some hundreds of millions of years.
The earth's crust has just settled and cooled sufficiently
to allow the germination of life. Don't ask how it
germinated. We will jump that difficulty, and assume the
appearance of some elementary self-propagating one-cell

organisms. That's all the living creatures there are. We will suppose them to be floating in water. Their only business is to feed themselves by wrapping themselves round and assimilating certain minute impurities in their liquid element – that, and, when mature, to split into two. Well now, are we going to say that all the forces and principles of action were then in position on earth, which were required to produce you and me? And if they weren't there, then where were they?

Whatever additional principles or powers have crept into the process have no doubt been fed in very gradually and indeed imperceptibly. But if one looks first at the beginning of the process and then at the end, how is one to deny that they have got fed in? Consciousness and choice, for example. I suppose we are to take it that our elementary cellular organisms lack these remarkable capacities. When, being in need of nourishment, they wash up against something assimilable, they just do wrap themselves round it by a reaction based on some sort of chemistry. To say that consciousness came in with infinite gradualness is not to deny that it was something radically new. Take an example from your own life. There was a time when you were not capable of philosophical reflection; now you are, for you are picking holes in my arguments. The difference is an absolute difference, but it has come about so gradually, you could not say when it began.

There is no difficulty in this case about seeing *how* the gradual development is brought about. Your parents were reflective animals, and they handed on to you a nervous system capable of the necessary functionings. Nor was that all. They themselves, and other reflective animals such as

schoolmasters, talked at you until you responded. They led
you through simple exercises in reflection until you got the
knack and did it for yourself. Not so primitive animal life,
nosing its way forward into consciousness. It develops
capacities which its ancestors had not. It has no teachers a
step or two ahead, to lead it on. It has no power to take
over the job of self-improvement, for it cannot see beyond
the end of its own nose.

"Well, but didn't Charles Darwin explain everything
without supposing any mysterious factors? All we need, he
said, is a tendency of living things to chance variation; and
who will deny that every living offspring, animal or vegetable, is slightly different from its brothers? So, in the
struggle for existence, the less useful variations will tend to
be eliminated, while the more serviceable establish themselves and hand down their inheritance."

Yes, and there is no doubt that this sort of thing happens.
But to say that it happens "by chance" is absurd. It happens
through the operation of the heredity-mechanism, which
acts in such a way that the results of chance variation or
selection are seized upon and put to use by vital function, en-
larging its scope; and in such a way that advantages thus
luckily acquired get built into the self-perpetuating pattern
of a stable species. The mechanism of heredity is already
partly known and is being intensively studied. No doubt it
will come to be as well understood as other biological
systems.

We may be tempted at this point to say "Then the evolutionary process is explained. Granted the mechanism of
heredity, and the common accidents of life, the result
simply follows." – "Granted the mechanism of heredity."

But how can it be taken for granted? The mechanism itself has to be accounted for. Before there was life, it wasn't there; and even when life began, it was not there in any developed form; it evolved along with the evolving species. "Granted that living things evolved a mechanism enabling them to evolve, there is no difficulty in seeing how they evolved." But there is some difficulty in seeing how they evolved the mechanism.

"Well, but they just did. And that's what life is like. Life isn't static, it grows – tentatively, gradually, blindly – and it throws up the systems or mechanisms its growth requires." As we declared some pages back about another dictum, "A very sensible remark" – if rightly understood. This is indeed how life behaves, when it has arrived on the scenes, and in proportion as it develops. The remark is a very fair general description; only it is not an explanation. We will follow our usual procedure, with which the reader must be by now familiar, and illustrate from a parallel case. Someone expresses astonishment at Shakespeare's capacity to collect ideas and images from every source, and melt them together into fire-new inventions. Someone else very reasonably comments, "Well, but that's how genius behaves." Only the comment is not an explanation. "Genius" is not a genie from *The Arabian Nights*, enslaved to the possessor of a magic lamp, and bound to fetch him ideas from the ends of the earth and to cook them up for him in a witch's cauldron. "Genius" is nothing but a name for the very ability which so astonishes us; and if someone says, "Well, that's how genius behaves" all he means is, "It's as astonishing as you like to call it, only it is not absolutely unique. Shakespeare could do it; but so in his own way could Virgil and, in very different fields, so could Aristotle, Newton and Einstein. We use the name 'genius' to describe this not very common sort of ability."

As with "genius", so with "life". If we say, "Well, life is like that" we are merely saying that there is some consistency in the evolutionary process all over the field of biological history; or perhaps we are saying that there is some analogy between the way in which an individual growth noses its way into its environment, and the way in which an extended process of biological evolution noses its way into its world. What we are not doing is supplying an explanation. And yet it is terribly tempting to suppose that we are. When we say of the evolutionary process "That's how life goes," we have to guard against false suggestion – the suggestion of a genie or daemon called "Life", with a customary programme of action ready worked out, which swoops down upon our earth as soon as the condition of the crust gives the magic sign, and proceeds to put the programme through. Any such suggestion is, of course, pure mythology, and misleading mythology at that. It disguises from our eyes the essential fact: the life-programme does not exist anywhere beforehand; it comes to be, is worked out, created, in the evolutionary process.

If you drain salt flats by damming out the tide, the action of rainwater will slowly but surely wash out the salt; and when the process has reached a certain stage, all sorts of plant-life will appear and quickly run riot. It is all too easy to think of the earth's surface on this model, in those days when it first cooled and settled. A point was reached when it provided a soil for life; and lo and behold! life proceeded to strike root, to grow and multiply. But the comparison is manifestly misleading. The plants which so suddenly appear on the salt-flats spring from seed dropped by birds or blown in by the wind; and the seed has built into it all the principles of growth required to give shape to its offspring. But no seed of life blew in from outer space to fertilize the earth; nor was there anywhere – or anyhow not anywhere relevant to earth's destinies – an already embodied and working set of principles laying it down how life should go on and build itself up.

I hope that enough has been said to show that the self-explanatoriness of the evolutionary process is very far from being a clear and simple truth. But the argument is of such importance, that I will resume it in another chapter, and hope to carry it a little further.

4

THE CREATION OF LIFE (II)

People, and not the most ignorant people either, will often say with assurance that in the unimaginable spread and multitude of stars there must be somewhere other planets in the state favourable to life as we know it on earth; and go on to say that if so, no doubt life has emerged there as it has here; indeed that there must have developed not only sentient but intelligent creatures.

It is worth pondering a little over the grounds for such a belief. Not, I mean, the belief that there are in the galaxies somewhere planets in some such state as our earth has attained. Not that; we may as well take that for granted. Not that belief, but the belief hung upon it; that the physical conditions will have thrown up the living creatures, not to say creatures headed towards a man-like intelligence. Why should we suppose anything of the sort? "Similar conditions are bound to produce similar consequences." Perhaps they are; but I'd dearly like to know why. "There is a law of nature to that effect." I dare say there is; only laws of nature don't float in the air. They are formulations of the ways in which real things act on, or react to, one another. The laws of nature are read off from the behaviour of existing beings. As more and more complex beings arise, they exhibit correspondingly more complex laws of behaviour. But where are those laws before the corresponding level of complexity has been reached? Where were the laws governing the operations of consciousness before anything was conscious? Don't tell me Dame Nature had them up her sleeve. There is no such sleeve and no such lady.

"Dame Nature, indeed! Don't be provocative. You know very well I should never suggest anything so childish. The laws governing the workings of consciousness were implicitly contained in the laws governing the operations of certain sorts of living tissue." I'm not sure that I like *implicitly contained in* much better than I like *Nature's sleeve*. It was for saying things like *implicitly contained in* that the medieval thinkers were cursed by the founders of modern physics. Still, don't let's be hasty; let's give *implicitly contained in* a run for its money. Only if we do, we shall have to have more of it. The principles of rational thought were implicitly contained in the principles of pre-rational animal behaviour and the principles of animal behaviour were implicitly contained in the reactions of pre-sentient animal bodies and the reactions of such bodies in the chemical reactions of cells and the reactions of cells in the functioning of inanimate substances – and to cut a long story short we come at last to the simplest, most elementary particle of energy, from which, we must suppose, all more complex forms or structures have in due course been built up. Clever little thing! It contained (implicity, of course) all the future developments of nature within it. I wonder how it managed to have enough folds in it to tuck away all those implications; for it was, in itself, such a simple little creature, with scarcely a wrinkle about it.

"Don't be absurd. You know perfectly well that a thing doesn't need to be complicated, to carry implications. Look at the number One. What can be simpler than One, the bare mathematical unit? And yet all the developments of mathematical structure are implicit in it." Well, yes, if you like to say so; but only *granted a mathematical intelligence of limitless capacity*, to work them out. Mathematical units are counters with which all the basic mathematical operations can be performed; and from those basic operations more advanced operations can be derived. But the operations do not perform themselves, nor do the derivations come of themselves. There has to be a mathematician. And if you are telling me that the basic units of physical nature are units out of which the whole complication of physical things, living or lifeless, can be built up, how can I help agreeing with you? Only it isn't news. We have still to find the builder. Bricks are standard elements out of which a limitless variety of buildings can be constructed. All the same, the bricks don't account for the buildings.

"It is easy to prove any case if you are allowed to pick your own analogies. Mathematical systems don't construct themselves, I admit; and why not? Because they are tissues of thoughts, and thought requires a thinker. Brick houses do not build themselves, either; and why not? Because bricks are passive materials made to be handled by builders. But the elementary systems out of which more complex systems arise by natural evolution are not passive material; they are patterns of energy in continuous action. For new systems to arise out of them, there is no need that superior agents should manipulate them from outside. Under given conditions, the forces themselves break into patterns of a new elaborateness. The new patterns get a hold, and establish themselves as running principles."

You are perfectly right; I am grateful to you for pointing out the misleading suggestions which my comparisons all too easily arouse. I did not, in fact, mean to draw any moral from the force required to pile up bricks into a house. What I had in mind was simply the fresh element of form or design that needs to come in. Sometimes when an elaborate piece of architecture is being put up in carved stone, the blocks come from the mason's yard so marked and numbered that their correct positions are unmistakable. If we chose to write a fairy tale about self-building blocks, and gave them the ability to climb into place and to lay themselves, we would have no difficulty over the self-erection of a structure of this kind. The pieces would swarm on to one another's backs and come to rest where the marks tallied. But now shoot a few cartloads of plain bricks down on a building site. Let them be as nimble as you like, how are they going to see their way into making one sort of house rather than another, or indeed any sort of house at all? A builder is needed, not to exert brute force and lift them into place, but simply to tap each one with the point of a magic trowel just when it's climbed where he wants it, so that it may know where to settle in. The builder can supply the form, for he has it in his head; so, of course, had the man whom we were supposing to have marked the prefabricated blocks in the mason's yard. But the cartloads of brick carry with them no form but the form of the brick; the form of the house is in no sense prefigured in the bricks, whether we take them one by one, or take them in the mass.

Perhaps my long-winded and somewhat childish parables cast little light on the matter. We might as well have stuck to the facts (always supposing that they are the facts). The scientific story begins with energy caught in elementary patterns and operating according to those patterns. It ends up with the same energy, caught in patterns of an almost limitless complexity and operating as the physical instrument of Shakespeare's wit or Newton's genius. From beginning to end of the story there is no need to suppose that any addition has been made to the quantity of energy employed; but the addition on the side of operative principle or pattern is surely staggering.

What we are trying to examine is the claim that the evolution of biological species, and in particular of man, can be accepted as self-explanatory on natural grounds. The task obliges us to consider what we mean by "natural explanation". Would anyone call it an explanation of any event, to demonstrate that there was present in the area of its occurrence sufficient physical energy to produce it? Obviously not. It needs to be shown that the energy was operating in patterns or along lines such as to give rise to the event.

Now if we take our primary physical systems which we suppose to lie at the root of the whole evolutionary process, can we say that they have in them the principles of action or the elements of pattern, sufficient to account for the end result? Manifestly not. Then what sort of explanation does the evolutionary hypothesis supply? Does it do more than show us that the new principles of form, though not prefigured in the primitive principles of physical organisation, are harmonious extensions to those principles; that they have been introduced very gradually, and always with perfect appropriateness to the conditions obtaining at each stage? Does the hypothesis give us any more than that?

"Yes, it does. It will be the endeavour of an evolutionary science to show not only that the new patterns of energy came in gradually and appropriately, but also that they came in inevitably. Wherever identical conditions are realised, science will claim that identical developments will follow. We do not merely suppose that some lifeless elements once long ago fused suddenly together into living cells, nor merely that it happened with a decent appropriateness, in view of the conditions then obtaining. We believe that if we can collect the same elements, and reproduce the conditions, it will happen for us tomorrow in the laboratory. It is a pity that the experiment has not yet been managed; but it would be rash for anyone to argue on the supposition that it never will be. It would be charming if we could hope to bring off similar experiments with the emergence of consciousness, by bringing a non-conscious organism up to the level at which consciousness dawns. But it is difficult to think of a test for the possession of elementary consciousness; and anyhow the experiment might take about a million years to carry through. But the difficulties are merely practical, and ought not to make any difference in theory. Consciousness, we must believe, never would fail to emerge where the development of biological reaction-pattern called for such an enhancement. And so with the other developments of evolutionary process."

I am happy to accept the correction. There is a great deal in the scientist's assumption that he could scarcely hope ever to prove; but it seems reasonable to let him have it. We ought to go with him in supposing that, under given conditions, new levels of complexity and new qualities of existence just do arise, and always would. But that is not to say that the new levels or the new qualities are the simple products of the conditions giving rise to them. It is merely to say that whatever powers or causes operate in producing them operate reliably. Since the new is not prefigured in the old, ought we not to suppose a Creator of what is new? All you are telling me is that he never misses his creative chances; he can be relied upon to act. But that is what I would expect of him, if indeed there is such a Being. Unlike me, of course. When the conditions are all set for me to act, I may not act. A free morning, a supply of pen, ink and paper, and this book to get on with, may still not lead to literary creation; I am in a bad mood or I have had a bad breakfast. But who can suppose such childish obstacles to beset the Creator of the world, or to stand in the way of his using his creative opportunities?

"If I may be allowed to say so, you have a perfect genius for dragging in parables to damage your own case. Only look at your latest effort in that line. When, after a breakfast good or bad, you overcome your native indolence and get down to your writing, the pen, ink and paper which you mention are the merest instruments of your activity. With the same pen, ink and paper you can write whatever you choose to write; whether it be letters to your friends or epigrams on your enemies, whether it be philosophical reflections or financial calculations, is all one to the pen, paper and ink. One might suppose that the Sovereign Creator (if there is any such person) would exercise at least an equal mastery and enjoy at least an equal freedom. But according to you, nothing of the sort – the state of the materials on which he puts his hand determines for him the nature of his next creative step."

As you say, parables keep on raising embarrassing suggestions, useful as they are in their way. If I liked, I could bluster it out with my parable of literary composition. I could make this sort of retort. When, conditions allowing, I sit down to go on with my writing, in nine cases out of ten I pick up the thread in the middle of an argument. And then I do not exercise an open freedom of choice as to what I do with pen, paper and ink. For if I am to make any sense of my work, I must carry the argument forward on its inevitable course. Now the God of Nature is not making fresh starts at every point in the evolutionary process; he is somewhere in the midst of the natural history which he is composing in the very stuff of life; and he will surely wish to continue it logically and consistently to the end. I could offer this sort of defence if I liked; but I think it is more genuine and more realistic to throw the parable over, and simply to point out that whereas a writer is playing with words, the God of Nature is creating things. How, then, might we expect him to proceed?

It will be useful to recall here what we said in the last chapter. Something over a century ago it was generally thought that there was a complete break between the creation of the natural order and the running of it, once it was created. God had made the system once and for all long ago; according to the Bible, he had made it in six days. Since then it had been running, and the running of it was acknowledged to be reliable and orderly, a proper subject for scientific study. People then had the same practical interest in the regularity of nature as they now have – they had to live with it, and they wanted to master it. But as for the supernatural acts of creation which were supposed once to have set it going, it did not matter how magical or how abrupt people conceived those acts to have been; for they were over and done with, there was no danger of mankind getting mixed up with them or having to cope with them.

Such, we said, was the old position. But Charles Darwin has changed all that, and fused the process of creation with the running of the natural order; for as we now see it, the work of creation is achieved through the way that nature runs. And what is the result? Not that the sequence of natural events becomes abrupt and magical in our view, but that creation becomes orderly, and of one piece with that system of events which science codifies. The progress of the creative work does not throw the natural order out of gear, nor fill it with irrational breaks, sudden starts, or unpredicted miracles. For then God would not be creating through the natural order, nor would he be the God of nature.

The same point can be put in a slightly different way. When people believed in a once-for-all creation on the first six days of time, they thought that the constituents of the world, once created, ran themselves. I do not mean by this that they thought things only needed God to get created and after that could do without him. They thought on the contrary, as believers have always thought, that every created thing needed the unceasing support of God's will. But God's will supported it in running itself after its own fashion. The world of things was not God's dream, neither was it God's puppet show, jerked into the semblance of vital action by heavenly wires. Things went by their own life, energy or momentum, according to the principles of action or of movement built into each of them. So thought our predecessors, and we cannot possibly go back on their conviction. What are we to say, then, when we find ourselves driven to admit that God creates things through the natural running of things? Shall we not be bound to say that he guides and supports them in their creating of themselves, and their creating of one another?

Hence the enormous slowness and, in a sense, the unlimited wastefulness of the evolutionary process. The creatures God carries through self-creation, or through world-creation, are elementary and stupid beyond expression – in fact they are beneath stupidity. Only a creature capable of intelligence can be called stupid. The principles of action built into them are so limited, so repetitive, that it takes an exposure to accident and an ordeal by trial and error over millions of years to achieve one or two creative steps.

"Forgive me for breaking in again – but aren't you sliding off the point? I thought we were discussing what reason there is for putting anything of a supernatural kind behind the evolutionary process. And here you are busy explaining why, if there's God behind it, he works through it in the way he does. But is there God behind it? That's the first question. May we please return to that?

"Perhaps it will help to get us back on to the track, if I summarise the part of your argument which seems to bear upon the main issue. That's simple. It all comes down to this. You say that the working principles of nature's organisation at any level are the working principles of organisation at that level, and cannot, by simply running or simply fulfilling themselves, do anything but keep that level of organisation or operation ticking over. They cannot account for, or sufficiently explain, the emergence of a higher level with its own higher principles. So you say. And do you want to know what I say to it? I say nothing to it. You see, it's not science. Scientists have nothing to do with 'explaining', or 'accounting for', the occurrence of anything in the way you mean. They do not ask whether there is a sufficient power, or a sufficient principle of action on the job to bring it about. They ask whether they can identify a set of conditions the overlapping or concurrence of which will always be followed by the sort of event they are talking about. If they can, they have done their job. The scientist is at bottom a practical, forward-looking man. He does not want so much to explain as to foretell. And for the purpose of prediction it is enough to know that given certain conditions a certain sort of result will follow. For then, where we see the conditions, we foreknow the result; and if we set the conditions, we produce the result. Of course the scientist studies the past, for what else is there to study? But he studies it for evidence of the way the world goes; and then he can hope to know what the future will bring."

I'm sure you are right. I do not want to contest a word that you say. All I have to remark is that science is not all. Scientists may not have anything to do with my "explanations" in so far as they are scientists, and nothing else. But scientists are also men; and men may have a concern with explanations.

"Men? If you mean 'men in general' I'm not too sure. A sustained interest in your ultimate explanations is rare enough. There are no doubt the speculative philosophers, technically called metaphysicians. But I have always suspected them of being a trifle mad."

Perhaps so. But may I be allowed to press you a little? Do you, or don't you, think that the sciences promise answers to all the questions we want to ask about the world?

"No, I don't. As I have heard you say yourself, all sciences are abstract – that is to say, they are selective. No science does more than pick out one sort of pattern from the workings of nature, and make that pattern as comprehensive and as consistent as it can. But the reality from which the patterns are picked is endlessly rich, mysterious and complex. Of course we can ask questions about it to which our sciences promise no answer, since none fathoms the depth or embraces the whole. We can ask our further questions – we may ask them, and answers may strongly suggest themselves. For instance, if we allow ourselves to dwell on this quest of yours for an ultimate cause, we may find much force in the arguments which point to a Creator. But – and this is the great 'But' in the whole matter – can we trust our minds, when they launch us so far into the deep?

"You might say that the success of science teaches us to trust the human intellect. Has not science been, from first to last, an enormous intellectual enterprise? Facts alone will teach us nothing, apart from the wit to interpret them and to draw consequences from them. Very true. Nevertheless scientists do not trust the intellect. They use it unsparingly but they do not trust it an inch. They use it to work out reasonable hypotheses. But nine reasonable hypotheses out of ten are wrong. Only fresh facts, directly observed, can show us which of our perfectly reasonable hypotheses will stand up. There was a time when scientists were content to go it on reason alone. Their arguments often did the highest credit to their abilities, but they got them nowhere. Since we have learnt to distrust mere reason and to submit to the arbitrament of fact, we have brought our ideas into so practical a correspondence with nature, that we are able to control her motions, or where we cannot control, predict. So we predict eclipses; we produce atomic explosions.

"I hardly need to draw the moral from my remarks. You can draw it for yourself. If mere reasoning runs off the rails in dealing with things so near to us as physical forces, we shall be mad to trust it on a matter so far removed from us and so deeply hidden as the Ultimate Cause. And so, as I said, we can certainly raise questions beyond the reach of science; but how are we to trust our answers? Unless, of course, we could obtain an experimental knowledge of God, and call our ideas to practical account."

Well, but that's just the point, isn't it? We do claim to have a practical knowledge of God. What do you imagine that we are discussing all this while? A pure question of theory, the mere satisfaction of our intellectual curiosity about the first origin of things? Of course not. If we are concerned about a Creative Cause, it is because, in creating all things, he is creating us; and it concerns us to enter into the making of our souls, and of one another's. To enter into the action of God thus is what we mean by religion; and as it is something we do, it is a matter of experience.

"Yes, I suppose that must be the point, if there is a point. But that will be a question for another day. Meanwhile I've a purely scientific query which wants clearing up. If I

understand the last twist of your argument, you are claiming that theology, though not a science, is something like a
science after all. It starts from the facts of the world, or of
nature, and it works out a hypothesis about a universal
cause. And the hypothesis is not left hanging in the air; it is
brought down to earth, applied to daily living, and in some
sense or other found to work.

"Very well. Now my difficulty is this. I think you claim
to be talking about a universal cause – a Being or a Will,
behind the unimaginable spread of stars which surrounds
us. Only you have taken as your main basis of argument
the development of life on this little planet. Apparently you
suppose that biological evolution here is typical of nature as
a whole; for if you do not think so, how can you make the
causing of it characteristic of nature's Creator, or argue
from it as though from a fair sample of his handiwork? I
take it, then, that you do think so. But on scientific evidence
you couldn't be more mistaken. So far as we know, the
evolution of life is an oddity peculiar to this tiny corner of
space which we occupy. Very likely there are other such
odd corners in other galaxies, but certainly not in such
number as to make them characteristic of the universe.
Life-bearing planets must be far rarer among stars than four-
leaved clovers in clover fields – not one in a million, the
veriest freaks and sports of nature. You have even less right
to call nature life-evolving than you have to call clover a
four-fingered plant.

"So much for the range of facts on which you base your
hypothesis. And now what about the range of experiment
you propose to test it upon? It extends no more widely
than human life. We men, you say, can experiment in a

moral co-operation with the creator of our souls. But you know you cannot teach dogs or cats to do it, let alone slugs or snails, not to mention vegetables or microbes. So where are you?

"You have a hypothesis about a universal Creator based on facts limited to a freak planet; and you experiment with it in a field narrower still, the behaviour of a single species: a species which, had lions developed an early taste for man-flesh, would never have survived to develop a religious sense. If ever there was a top-heavy hypothesis, this is it. Won't you cut your losses and tailor your hypothesis to fit your facts? Won't you be content to talk about a creator of plants and animals, not of galaxies? Even then your experimental verification remains absurdly narrow; it will only support you in postulating a creator of moral persons."

Are these your difficulties? You seem to have forgotten the steps by which we got on to evolutionary ground. Hadn't we been talking about astronomy? It is not true that we proposed to see God's creative action in biological evolution alone. So far as we were able to look at astronomical realities, they appeared as brute facts, in need of explanation; an explanation lying outside themselves, in some shaping Power. Since the scale and the sketchiness of astronomical knowledge proved so baffling, we decided to see nature taking shape in a more accessible area; and so we picked evolution on this planet. We did not take it as a typical sample of nature's structure-building, but as a range from which we could argue downwards on to levels which are truly typical of the universe as a whole. For there seemed no reason whatever for supposing that nature's structure-building begins where life begins. On the contrary, our evidence is that lifeless matter consists of energy caught in patterns of a less or greater complexity. And if there is indeed a creative Power which weaves up the tissue of living things, there is every reason to suppose that the same Power has woven the physical web from the very bottom and made all the stuff of the universe.

The point that arises out of your second grievance is really the same point. You say that we take God to be a *universal* cause. But a universal Cause in this connexion is not simply a Cause of which the action covers the whole field, it is a Cause which does the same thing for everything in the field it covers – that is, creates it. The differences are all on the side of the creature – they are differences in the thing created. If any creature can experiment in co-operation with the Creative Will, it touches creation – it touches the action which is the only cause with an unlimited scope. It is pointless to object that only a creature with the necessary gifts can make the crucial experiment. The experiments of physics or of chemistry are not called in doubt because they cannot be carried out by dogs or cats, not to name slugs or snails. Man is the scientist, just as man is the worshipper. If there are angels, no doubt they are better worshippers, and better scientists too. The brutes are neither. A scientist is concerned with a certain range of created realities, and his test experiments should sample that range. A worshipper is concerned with the Creative Power, and it is enough if he can co-operate with it where it touches him.

5

THE GOD OF NATURE

It is often suggested that there are two approaches to belief in God. We may reason from the world to a divine Cause, or we may trust religious experience. What I have just been saying will have been said in vain, if my readers still think that the two paths run separate. The practice of religion is what brings to life our reasonings about the world's ultimate Cause, and gives reality to them; while on the other side our reasonings about the world give sense and definiteness to a religious faith in God. It isn't a choice between following the reason and trusting the heart. It is a matter of putting heart into a rational conviction, and bringing mind into the heart's devotion. Theism is not an emotional attitude; there is hard thinking behind it, and sound reasons of which the believer has no cause to be ashamed, in any company. We should not let ourselves be browbeaten by people who take natural science to be the sole method for establishing truths of fact or of existence, and who refuse to let the scientific quest for knowledge extend beyond the boundaries of the sciences themselves.

Religious conviction stands on the two feet of reason and experience. No doubt there are believers in plenty who accept their religion from their predecessors in faith, and find assurance in practising it, without having ever reasoned out a single argument about the Cause of the World.

But the rational conviction is there. The simpler they are in their faith, the more rocklike will be their belief in "God the Father Almighty, Maker of heaven and earth". Since they were first told that "things did not make themselves", that proposition has spoken to their minds as an evident truth. There are plenty of convictions which are profoundly reasonable, and of which the force may be felt without any long process of argument; yet they need a long argument to establish them, once they are called in question. Another example is the truth that a man's choice is free, so that he can be held responsible for his voluntary acts. A sound and simple mind does not question it, yet what a tangle of argument it raises, once it is challenged!

So the practical believer has his share of rational conviction, even though he has never reasoned it out. But if he never does, he lies open to a serious danger, the danger of tacking on to his religious belief a deal of discreditable nonsense; and if he trails it about with him, sooner or later he will trip over it. If we think about the God of personal salvation only, and take the Cause of nature for granted, we shall be for ever misunderstanding the natural workings of God.

The misunderstanding comes about in the following way. In his personal dealings with us, God's action is personal, and not only personal, but human. He makes himself like us in coming to meet us. If we know God in no other way, we shall incline to see him as equally human in his handling of nature. And so, without noticing what we are doing, we shall keep imagining that his purposes in the material world are such as ours might be. We men are constantly trying to humanise our environment and fit it to our minds. We cultivate the fields, we plan the landscape, we domesticate our fellow-creatures, we process materials, we build houses and we construct machines. Even where we leave our environment untouched by our hands, we want to get it into our heads; and that means fitting unruly facts into the sort of neat schemes men can master. Why, our very eyes are up to the same game. I go into a scene of wild mountain splendour. My reaction to it may not be to *think* about it at all. I may not attempt, for example, to understand the geological formation or to guess the altitudes. I may simply feast my eyes upon it. I call it beautiful; for whichever way I look, the most interesting arrangements of masses and colours, of light and shadow present themselves. There are a hundred lovely pictures in the panorama. But they are all in the eye of the beholder. It is my eye that draws the scene together into views, and it is the views that are beautiful. Not that the beauty lies in my eye alone. It lies in the materials which the mountains offer to my vision, and in their adaptation to my sense for pattern – for pattern, and for whatever other elements go to the make-up of aesthetic delight.

If I am a pious man, there may be nothing that more readily moves me to the praise of my Creator than the contemplation of such a scene. I worship the God of beauty. Human skill, I tell myself, is proud to have arranged a single pattern of aesthetic charm on a few feet of painted canvas; divine contrivance has set a whole landscape in everlasting rock, in rushing torrents and in springing trees. And in telling myself this I do not err. That adaptation of my eye to environment, and of environment to my eye, which produces aesthetic delight, is a masterpiece of God's skill. Not only has he created man, he has fitted him to his environment in a hundred subtle ways; among which not the least remarkable is this relation of things to our eye, giving aesthetic delight, and sometimes ecstasy.

Only I must beware of over-humanising, or of taking the comparison between God and the painter too far. The painter thinks of nothing but the picture. He is interested in the paint and canvas solely for the way they can be made to look. What their chemical composition may be, what active processes are going on in the atoms that make them up, is of no concern to him. He is merely careful to select materials which will place no obstacles in his way, nor do anything to cramp his liberty in painting. If then I allow myself to think of God as an artist in living landscape, I shall wonder why he uses materials which are so largely irrelevant to his purpose, so frustrating; and I shall notice that, while some of his works are supremely beautiful, some are humdrum to the eye, some hideous and discordant; as though his materials had got out of hand and defeated his artistry.

What is my mistake? I have forgotten that God is the Cause of the world's existence, and that he has woven nature up from the bottom. That natural beauty which is such a charm in my eyes is, as it were, a divine afterthought; a sweet enjoyment for mankind in the look of a world whose existence serves quite other ends. Scenic beauty belongs to the sphere of man, and man was a late arrival. The masses of the mountains were not trimmed for human eyes; landscape is not a landscape-garden. God's goodness is not disappointed because not all scenes are equally lovely to us. God does not form ideal projects and regret to find them imperfectly realizable. He rejoices that rocks and trees, rivers and meadows, created on quite other principles, afford such feasts to human eyes; as indeed he rejoices that vegetables and beasts, created for their own sakes, afford a necessary food for human stomachs.

However often I remind myself not to be so absurd, I fall back into imagining that God begins with human purposes about his sub-human creations; and that he puts a constraint upon himself to let them be their brainless sub-human selves, and go their brainless sub-human ways. But what folly that is! God does not think of sub-human things humanly. The natural world is not a mere physical show, behind which there stands a scaffold of manlike planning. The physical world does not *look* physical, it *is* physical, and its Creator thinks it or means it just as it comes.

It is a poor speaker of French who thinks in English and translates as he goes; the true master of tongues thinks as he talks. He is a Frenchman in France and a German in Germany; why, he may find himself dreaming in German or in French. The shape, the idiom of the Creator's thought is the very shape and idiom of his creature's existence. God's thought of man is human, for he thinks man as he is. It is true that his thought of man stretches man, and reaches out into possibilities undreamt by us; but these possibilities are still human. God's thought for us extends into the heaven he has prepared for us; but heaven itself is a human state; it is the state of man-in-glory. God's thought of lions is lionlike, and of sparrows sparrow-like; and elementary things that have neither life nor sense are thought and willed by him exactly as they are or as they go.

I am not denying that the mind of man is a better image

of God's mind than the mind of a beast, not to say than the mindless striving of inanimate forces. Only the divine quality in the human mind is not its humanness but its sheer mentality: its power (a limited power, certainly) to escape from ways of thought which express the human attitude, and to see every sort of thing just as it is.

One of the fascinating topics of space-fiction is the meeting of minds reared on different planets, and attached to utterly different species of animals. If man meets Martian, and the Martian has attained to the use of reason, communication will (we rightly suppose) be somehow established between us. And why? Because in spite of all difference in natural sentiment or in spoken idiom, both will have some power of talking objectively about the same things; for instance, they may compare notes on commonsense astronomy. They will meet and mutually understand, just in so far as their speech expresses something neither Martian nor human, but objectively factual. That will be the starting-point. But we cannot be content to think of their going no farther. The man goes on to get some understanding of the Martianness of the Martian, and the Martian to get some understanding of the humanness of the man. And so man and Martian think together when they are both thinking about the Martian, for both are thinking Martianly; and equally together when both are thinking about the man; for then both are thinking humanly.

Perhaps we shall never meet Martians, but we have about us creatures of other kinds into whose bosoms we can dive and out of whose eyes we can peep. We are not utterly without a sense of how a cat or a dog experiences its world. Not utterly without, but the power is painfully limited in us.

Not utterly without, for we have mind, and mind (so far as we have it) is divine. And God can think every created existence, just as it goes. Indeed it would neither go like that nor be like that, if God did not think it so.

Yet people commonly imagine that believing in God means pretending that the world of nature is what it plainly is not – the expression of manlike planning; only that God uses materials so awkward and so unruly that they would defeat us entirely; but he displays infinite patience in waiting for them to shake down at last into something like the lines of his grand design. What an unreasonble supposition! God thinks things as they are and designs them to go the way they go. He does not impose an order against the grain of things; he makes them follow their own bent and work out the world by being themselves. It is no matter of regret to God that the universe is not a piece of streamlined engineering. It is meant to be what it is – a free-for-all of self-moving forces, each being itself with all its might, and yet (wonder of wonders!) by their free interaction settling into the balanced systems we know, and into the complexities whereby we exist.

The seemingly free action of nature is not a put-up job. The Creator of the world is not to be compared with those bad novelists who make up the plot of their story first, and force the characters to carry it out, all against the grain of their natures. He is like the good novelist who has the wit to get a satisfying story out of the natural behaviour of the characters he conceives. And how does he do it? By identifying himself with them and living them from within. There are no stage villains in a good novel, and no plaster saints either. The storyteller can make his people as good or as bad as he likes, but only if his heart can go with them in being as good or as bad as he makes them.

It is a formidable task to work a novel on a wide canvas, creating characters in various social relationships and various bundles of kindred, with a political setting and a geographical scene all complete, the whole vividly presented and adding up to a consistent story. The detail is never entirely worked out; the most exacting reader does not ask that even from Tolstoy or from Trollope. Characters from outside the story can walk into it and create disturbances, without our expecting to be told who their grandmothers were or what sort of childhood they had. The hero can fall ill, without our demanding a history of the microbes which infected him, or of the blood-corpuscles which failed to master the microbes. He can beget a child with a snub-nose, without our requiring an account of the genes which determined the child's physical inheritances. He can walk into a dramatic thunderstorm, without the support of a week's weather-charts covering the Atlantic and the North Sea. In short, we are content if we can see that the principal characters *would* behave in the circumstances as they are shown to behave. We do not wish to see that the circumstances *would* turn out so – that the fever would take that course or the thunder break at that hour. The author must have got truly inside a certain number of his people; his thought need not have lived its way through every natural process, whether minute or vast, which he supposes to come to bear on them.

What is an impossible task for the human author is a constant achievement with the Author of Nature. He thinks all the natural processes at any level into being themselves and into running themselves true to type. And yet without faking the story or defying probability at any point he pulls the history together into the patterns we observe. The novelist who depicts the running of a business must manage it without reducing the office underlings to automata; he must allow them the free play of their personalities. God's creative thought must go deeper; while he thinks out the orderly life of a man's mind, he must at the same time think out the action of the minute physical underlings which carry the work of his brain, as they act out their own destinies according to their kind. If they are to do so, it must sometimes be that they rebel; the brain misfunctions or incurs damage, the purposes of thought are frustrated. Sometimes it must be so. Yet most of us are sane and capable most of the time, by Heaven's grace.

What moves believers to worship moves atheists to ridicule. A thought living at once on every level of natural process and thinking all levels into a single story is to believers the wonder of omnipotence and to sceptics the height of absurdity. Perhaps we cannot make those who come to scoff at us remain to pray with us. It will be something if we can help those who come to pray, pray with a more understanding adoration.

Before we let our account of the Creative Mind be written off as impossible or absurd, we can point out that it embodies the ideal after which our own thought strives and which in some slight measure it even realises. We have to specialise and to select, we have to take our world to pieces level by level in order to find our way in it; and yet we know all the time that what we take apart belongs together; and we make some effort to see the various levels of nature's action in one view, when we have finished our selective inquiries into one at a time. While we are working out political or economic statistics it will be difficult for us to consider the voters or market-operators we are counting, as free moral persons. Yet that is what they are, and when we pause for breath in our calculations we can make some effort to realise them as such. While we are thinking of men as characters, or as moral agents, we can scarcely be considering them as physical animals, systems of uncountable cells where each cell has its own vital action. But that (again) is what they are; and when we have leisure for it, we try to capture the wholeness of vision, physical and spiritual.

We cannot think with effect on all levels at once; we recognise that it would only be by so thinking that we could see things as they are. Such efforts as we actually make to round off and balance our view are neither more nor less than efforts to approach the thought which believers attribute to God. And since the effort to think as many-sidedly as we can is not a fantastic or a futile enterprise, but the very road of sober truth, we can scarcely condemn as fantastic a doctrine which allows the divine mind to achieve what even we attempt. We are merely saying that God *knows* – for this is what proper knowing would be.

One of the reasons which makes God's universal knowledge seem incredible to us is that we imagine him as having all those obstacles to surmount which stand in the path of human knowledge. There is only one sort of process that I quite simply and immediately understand; and that is the thing I myself mean and do. All other processes or activities that go on in the world are approached by me through their outside effects, and more or less laboriously put together in my mind with the aid of much talk and many diagrams. Even then it is seldom I can feel the nerve of the process I sketch to myself. Think what an agony it is to put together any conception of what goes on within the atom. One is struggling all the time to escape from being human so as to think atomically; and it can't be done.

It cannot be like that with God. God does not have to escape from being divine so as to understand his creatures; nor does he have to reconstruct them bit by bit on the evidence of their outside effects. As I was saying just now, I myself have a direct understanding of the thing I mean and do. But the active existences of created beings are all things that God directly means and puts into effect; for that is what is meant by calling him the Creator of them. How then can God fail to know them directly, and from the inside? Are they not bound to go as his thought of them goes? They spread the field of their activity, they make contact with the action of other beings. God's thought spreads through them, and at the same time through the beings with which they make the contact. He feels from both sides the interplay of forces; and so he understands it for what it is.

Once we have grasped the simplicity and the directness of God's thought, we may fairly ask ourselves whether the marvel of it really adds anything to the marvel of the world itself, the world which he thinks. For God's thoughts and the real processes composing the world perfectly correspond. The universe is unbelievably multiple and many-levelled, and yet makes up a single whole of interactions;

a whole so far from being merely chaotic, that it allows the development of relatively stable systems, and of that physical being we men enjoy. God's thought of the world is equally multiple and equally many-levelled. He thinks the world together into a whole; but it is into the same whole as it physically composes. The whole complexity of the world is in the divine mind, yes; but the whole complexity of the world is also in the world; and it is the same complexity.

An unbeliever says: "The complexity of the world is quite enough to swallow. That it should be the double of a divine thought, doubles the dose. It's too much for my stomach to take." A believer replies: "The complexity's not doubled at all. One and the same complexity issues out of the divine will and gives shape to the world. By dropping out the divine thought you do not halve complexity, you take away explanation. How are we to swallow the world's achievements of pattern, as results due to no influence and proceeding from no cause?"

There is, of course, this difference between God's thought of the world, and the world's own order: the pattern is scattered piecemeal over the forces or events which make up the world; it is drawn together and enjoyed as one in the mind of God. In this respect the divine mind is like the human. A human botanist grasps and possesses the "family" structure of plant-classification. The pattern is there, figured in the facts of plant-life; but it is nowhere drawn together, collected and possessed, but in the mind of the botanist. In an old-fashioned botanical garden, like our Physick Garden at Oxford, the attempt is made to play the botany back on to the plants, by bedding them in order, according to Linnaeus's classifications. Flowers and pedantry go oddly together, and we smile to see rosaceae all in one border and compositae in another. Yet even here all that is done is to make nature's pattern plainer to the students' eye. Though umbelliferae are cheek by jowl with umbelliferae, they do not know their neighbourhood. It is nothing to them that they are cousins, now they are next door, any more than it was when they flourished in different continents.

So the whole system of nature is neither drawn together nor realised in the world, but only in the wisdom of God. To any genuine believer, the truth of this is incontestable; and yet even this opens a pitfall for the imagination. As soon as we conceive this drawing together of multitude in the focus of a single view, our fancy calls up a solitary figure such as our botanical student, standing at a corner of the border, and running his eye over the umbelliferae or the compositae. The species scattered over the extent of the bed are brought together at a single point of space, in one brain, by one pair of eyes. And just as the eyes cannot take in every plant at once, but can only keep them under review by chasing up and down, so the brain can only support the thought of one kind at a time, and for thinking of many together must have recourse to vagueness or to generalisation.

With some such human model in mind we turn to the thought of God's wisdom, and of how it draws the universe into the focus of a single view. We shall naturally allow that God's capacity for seeing or thinking many things at once is much greater than ours; yet the idea of its being *infinitely* greater carries no conviction. How can we seriously believe that God can have time or attention for every detail in this impossibly vast and endlessly complex universe? Every circumstance, indeed, may be "naked and open to the eyes of him with whom we have to do", if he chooses to turn his eyes that way. But surely he cannot choose to bestow his attention equally in all directions at once.

So we imagine; and why? Because we have been trapped by an inadequate comparison. We have compared the drawing together of the universe in the universal Mind with the drawing together of the universe in one detail of itself, one human person. And obviously the whole cannot be adequately focused in one of its minutest parts. If we must have a comparison to help us, let's try another. People used long ago to call God "the Soul of the World". By employing this expression, they compared God's presence in the universe with my conscious presence in my own body. I am so present in every bodily part that I have some feeling of it; I think it unnatural that anything much should happen to any part of me, without my being aware of it. Said the ancients in their own phrase, "The soul extends all through the body, yet the soul is one." It is admittedly true that I am not equally attentive to the feel of every part of my body at any one time; the spotlight of attention wanders up and down with the interest of the moment, sometimes picking out my hand, sometimes my foot, and sometimes a foolish little tickle in the small of my back. But bodily feeling is everywhere there, and it is mine, even when I am not specially attentive to it.

Following this analogy, we may conceive that God's mind feels through all the world, since everything in it is his work, so how could he be unaware of it? It would be contrary to the nature of things for him to be so. We shall not, perhaps, find it too great a strain on our imaginations to take out of our picture of God one feature in our picture of ourselves: the little spotlight of attention bobbing about. God cannot need specially to attend; he knows up every nerve. Is not that at least half of what is meant by calling God's mind *infinite*? A finite mind has a limited capacity of attention. Just as my arms can manage only a certain number of parcels, and must drop some to take up more: so I must disattend from some things, to have attention for others. How it vexes me, alas!, when I am attending to my writing, and they tear my attention away from it, to attend to household affairs! I fear they have a sad time of it; they might as well try to tear a bone from a bulldog. We cannot suppose that God is either obsessed by one thing, or distracted by many; everything is present to his knowledge just by existing in his world.

It is not true, of course, that we men can never think of more than one thing at a time. I can chat to a neighbour while I carry on a job of carpentry. It need not even be true in any damaging sense that in such a case I attend in either direction "with only half my mind". That is the sort of thing I might say in apology, if it were afterwards pointed out to me that I had made a stupid remark in the conversation, or a blunder in the woodwork. "Sorry, I had only half my mind on it." But if the subject of conversation is familiar and the carpentry straightforward, I may well have for either occupation all the attention it requires. Perhaps in the course of the conversation I give a decision about some matter, and perhaps it turns out unfortunately. I should like to be able to excuse myself by saying that I only gave the matter half my mind. But I may know perfectly well that the excuse would be insincere. Carpentry or no carpentry, I gave the business all the attention it demanded; and if my hands had lain idle in my lap, I should have given the same decision. I understood the issue and I applied my standing policy about such things. It was the true answer of my mind, not of half my mind. To put it simply, it was my decision; it was I.

So it may be, even with us men. It should not be too difficult, then, for us to see that God does not act with a mere fraction of his mind at any one point in his creation. I do not mean (how could I?) that every detail of his work is sufficient to fill and absorb an infinite mind. I mean that whatever he thinks is what he wholly intends, that there is no more to be thought about it beyond what he thinks, and that it could receive no fuller attention, were he to disattend from everything else.

We may say, then, that God's mind lives in all the world as my feeling "soul" lives in my whole body or, to put it in antique terms, that God acts as the Soul of the World. It is better, by the way, to say "*acts* as the Soul of the World" than to say "*is* the Soul of World". For if we say "is", we seem to be confining God's action to the world he indwells or animates. When we say that the consciousness, or feeling-soul of any animal *is* the soul of that animal, we mean that its essential function is to animate that one body. We understand the "soul" and its bodily house or instrument to have grown up together; or if either came first, it was the bodily system. Is there not some rudiment of an animal there, before consciousness dawns in it? All of this is implied in saying that the consciousness *is* the consciousness, or the soul, of the animal in question. And we cannot want to say any of this about God in his relation with the world he animates. To suggest that he is tied to the world-system in any such fashion is to make nonsense of our whole discovery of the divine. Our minds feel after God as creator and cause of whatever system there is in the world; and to be this he must stand above it, and come before it. If God's thought thinks the world into being, his mind cannot essentially *be* the soul of that world. But we may say that in making it, he acts as its Soul, by feeling (or knowing, rather) along every nerve of the world-process he creates.

It must follow from all we have been saying in this chapter, that wherever we come up against the living process of nature, we meet the thought and will of God. Not in the gross and outward show of things, with which they strike our senses; but in the intimate process of activity by which they are themselves. In so far as our science strips away the sensory show and lays bare the rhythm of active being, it approaches the divine creative thought.

Is the natural scientist, then, a natural theologian? He may be or he may not. We have known scientists whose direct contact with the physical reality was a constant motive for religious awe. But it may not be so. In every branch of human activity, and in science not the least, there is scope for pride and for the sense of power. The scientist can do his work without ever giving a moment to the contemplation of the vital existences with which he is in touch. The object before his mind may be his own diagram, theory, or experiment; his concern may be with intellectual mastery, with success. But then the same thing may be true of a biblical scholar. He may be so obsessed with his own cunning in solving problems of interpretation, or working out connexions in the history of ideas, as to have no feeling for the movement of the Spirit in the life of God's people.

Though by thinking we approach the work of God, the work of God is never just what we think: there is a point at which we have to stop being clever about things, and let things be themselves, not the pretty diagrams our minds make of them. If we do let them be themselves, they will be what our thought never quite overtakes. It is as foolish to think we have got to the bottom of nature, as it is to think we have got to the bottom of our fellow-men. The works of God are not irrational, they are endlessly intelligible; but that means there is always more and more for us to understand in them.

The way to study God's mind in nature is to let things show us how they go. No doubt God's providence will also work their natural action into higher designs; but we have seldom any reason to trust our guesses as to what these higher designs may be. Those who start from a rash confidence in such guesses, instead of starting from a patient study of natural processes, land themselves in that terrible morass of muddled thinking which goes by the name "the problem of suffering". If an earthquake shakes down a city, an urgent practical problem arises – how to rescue, feed, house and console the survivors, rehabilitate the injured, and commend the dead to the mercy of God; less immediately, how to reconstruct in a way which will minimise the effects of another such disaster. But no theological problem arises. The will of God expressed in the event is his will for the physical elements in the earth's crust or under it: his

will that they should go on being themselves and acting in
accordance with their natures.

"But does not God overrule natural forces for higher
ends?" – Overrule? And what is overruling? "The local
authority gave permission for the siting of a petrol-station
in front of the waterfall, but the Ministry overruled the decision." In plain terms, the superior authority stopped the
mayor, aldermen and councillors doing a nice little job for
a friend. They did not abolish, or challenge, the right of
these worthies to give such permissions in general; but at a
point where their action conflicted with public policy in regard to natural amenities, they stepped in and coerced the
mayor and council. It is anyhow sufficiently obvious that
God does not overrule in this way. He does not let natural
forces have their heads up to the point only at which their
free action would conflict with some fixed principle of
higher purpose, for example the welfare and safety of mankind, nor does he, when that point is reached, substitute
miracle for nature and stop physical forces from indulging
in their characteristic behaviour.

What would happen to the system of nature if God did
habitually overrule, is too terrible to contemplate. Fortu-
nately he does not overrule; he uses, or in some mysterious
way persuades. Does God use the crust and undercrust of
the earth for man's benefit? Does he lead or persuade
physical elements present there into structural combinations
on which human life is built? Certainly; that is just what he
does do – always supposing that there is a God of nature at
all. The success of biological life requires that the earth's
crust should for the most part have cooled and settled. If
the process had gone so far that there was no risk either of

earthquake or volcano, it might be too cool for us altogether; snow and ice would win the day, as no doubt they
will at last, when there has been enough of human history.

"Are you denying, then, that a particular earthquake or
a particular eruption plays any part in God's further purposes?" – No, I am not denying it. God works everything
into his further purposes, for his work never ceases; and he
always goes on from the actual situation into which things
have come. Everything gets worked into God's further
purposes. So God brings much good out of much evil;
much good that we cannot recognise, but a considerable
range that we can. The flow of lava which drives the vil-
lagers from their cottages will enrich their fields, as it
crumbles, with an unparalleled fertility. The earthquake
which destroys the town calls forth in some victims heroic
virtue and teaches others to know their own weakness.
People in the surrounding cities are shaken out of their
usual selfishness and give so much in relief that they halve
their cigar-smoking, or put off the purchase of a shinier car
for eighteen months; a moral triumph indeed.

It cannot be disputed that such sorts of good are born out
of disaster; but the disaster is a disaster still. Healthy and useful lives are lost to the earth. Earth's loss is heaven's gain, no
doubt; but couldn't heaven have waited? Sane people for-
feit their reason, cripples linger on, horribly maimed;
to save their lives or their possessions, decent men com-
mit acts of unspeakable meanness, which stain their conscience for the rest of their lives; some become embittered,
some can never find their feet again when the ground
on which they so comfortably stood is cut from under
them.

It is not, then, that the humanly inconvenient by-products of volcanic fire are cushioned or diverted; it is not that all harms to man are prevented. It is that the creative work of God never ceases, that there is always something his Providence does, even for the most tragically stricken. There is always a will of God to be sought in any situation, however unpromising – to be sought by our minds, that it may be served by our hands. I will not bring forward in this connexion the Christian's sheet-anchor – the assurance that Providence is never ultimately defeated because God raises the dead. For that is not a prospect which opens before the eyes which look for God in the workings of nature. We must look in another direction to learn of that.

The question of Providence and suffering is endless. It presents a separate problem in every case, for in every case the special redeeming Purpose has to be looked for or waited for. I do not mean to discuss such cases here, for where should I begin and where should I stop? I have merely wished to show the bearing of the problem on my present theme. The volcanic eruption, taken in itself, shows the Creative Mind thinking physically, not humanly. For the divine thought identifies itself with nature at every level on which nature operates.

If I am challenged to say in one sentence why there are what men call natural disasters, I shall say this: it is because God makes the world make itself; or rather, since the world is not a single being, he makes the multitude of created forces make the world, in the process of making or being themselves. It is this principle of divine action that gives the world such endless vitality, such vital variety in every part. The price of it is, that the agents God employs in the basic levels of the structure will do what they will do, whether human convenience is served by it or not. Yet the creative persuasion has brought it about that there is a world, not a chaos, and that in this world there are men.

Would it have been possible for God to have made a world without a free-for-all of elemental forces at the bottom of it? I suppose not, but I do not know; and there is (I take it) only one Mind that does. Without answering any such question, I can be convinced that this actual self-making world of ours expresses the will of a Creator; and equally without answering it, I can thank God heartily for my existence.

6

EXPERIMENTAL PROOF

It is a popular attitude nowadays even with professed believers to wallow in theological indecision and in particular to refuse to affirm anything about the personal nature of God. But if belief does not assert that everywhere and in all things we meet a sovereign, holy and blessed Will, then what in the world does it assert? If we don't mean this, let us confess ourselves atheists, and stop confusing the public mind.

One of the reasons for muddled talk about the non-personality of God is the important truth we discussed in the last chapter; I mean, that God thinks physically, not humanly, about physical things. But to think physically does not make the thinker impersonal; it takes a personal being to think physically or, indeed, to think anyhow. The doctrine of the non-personal God really amounts to this: there is a nature-like power at the bottom of nature, a power which becomes human when nature throws up man. Man himself, to be precise, is distinctively human, or personal, on his highest levels only; the power which expresses itself in our bodily or animal nature has not yet taken on the personal form.

The proper epithet for this system of ideas is "superficial". It does not wade in deep enough to be the slightest use. It recognises that God works impersonally at an impersonal level, but it fails to recognise that it is God who so works. It is useless as theory or explanation, because there is no meaning at all in the notion of a non-personal power working nature. What does the non-personal power add to nature itself? The natural world is a tissue of impersonal powers, or forces, working away like mad; and what is added to the story by throwing in non-personal Power with a big P? The doctrine is equally useless as religion; for why should I go down on my knees to this cosmic Juggernaut or pay it the least respect? It is not as good a man as I am. We know we have to put up with nature, and that we can master it only by obeying it; but it's a long step from that to worshipping it.

What Christians must think is that God, in himself, is supremely personal; that in his creation of the world the activities he thinks physically come before those he thinks biologically, not to say personally; but that where God's creation does reach the personal level, there results a creature who can think back through the physical to the personal Cause; that is, to God.

If we ask whether nature reveals God, the answer will be Yes and No. Yes, for nature presents us with a vast extent of God's physical and creative thought; it gives us evidence for the enormous scope and intimate subtlety of his wisdom. No, for nature fails to supply the essential clue by which her own signs can be read; the notion of wisdom or of mind itself. We must look to mankind for that. But once granted it is mind that weaves the natural world, the woof becomes evidence of the weaver's artistry.

The world-order on the one hand, and human mentality on the other, suggest to us the hypothesis that wisdom made

the world, and supply us with the terms in which to
formulate it. But what can test or prove the hypothesis?
What will give us the right to affirm it? Our scientific
background leads us to ask for experimental evidence, as
we said at the beginning. Is theology a science? We asked;
and we concluded, No, not a science as other sciences are.
But, we said, not unscientific either, nor even unscience-
like. Inquiries which begin in the scientific field may jump
the fence into theological speculation. Moreover theological belief has a sort of practical evidence, through which
it is put to the test. Theology is no more up in the air than
physics; people act upon both. We must now turn to this
experimental (or as-it-were-experimental) element in the
"Science of God".

Probably most people nowadays suppose that it is quite a
modern question, whether theology is a science, and if so a
science of what sort. If they suppose this they are mistaken.
The issue was debated with much acuteness seven hundred
years ago. In his discussion of it St. Thomas Aquinas made
a remark so decisive that I must have it; and rather than
steal it without acknowledgement, I prefer to give credit
where credit is due. There are two sorts of science, he says,
the contemplative and the practical. The aim of contemplative science is the sheer satisfaction of knowing, whereas
practical science studies things we can work. Now it may
look, says the Saint, as though theology were a practical
science, since it sets us to work right enough on works of
charity and of religion. Nevertheless, the principal subject
of theological study is God. And we cannot work God; on
the contrary, we men are God's work. And so, concludes
the Saint, theology is primarily a contemplative science.

The flat distinction between contemplative and practical knowledge belongs to a bygone age and it is not this that I want to take up. All I want is contained in the sentence "Practical science studies things we can work. But God is not to be worked by us; on the contrary, we men are God's work". It is the happiness of a certain sort of genius to put profound truths in words so few and so clear, that they have the force of axioms; there's no more to be said, it seems. But the next step St. Thomas takes does not carry the same conviction: theology is more concerned to look at God than to do anything about him. It is open to us to draw a different moral. There *is* a practical relationship, for though God is not our work, we are his; and some of the work he does in us employs our own hands.

If we want to think straight about the parallel between natural sciences and science of God, this is the point to seize. Is there anything in religion resembling experiment? Yes; only the person who does the experiment is God. It is God's doing, his work on us; not our doing, not our work on him. It is not, however, God's *experiment*; its experimental value is for us. God does not experiment, for what is an experiment? It is a practical manipulation serving as a crucial test for the soundness of a general hypothesis. The concern of the experimenter is not with the experiment but with the hypothesis it is to check. But we cannot think that God's concern with us is to prove general truths out of us. We read in the Book of Job how a good man's devotion is put to the test. No one, surely, who studies the book supposes its lesson to be that the individual's sufferings allow the Almighty to verify a hypothesis: "The worshipper of God worships him for what he is, not for what he gives."

There are two monstrosities in the suggestion. The first is that God needs to prove general truths if he is to be assured of them; the second is that he is concerned with generalization, not with Job. It is Job who stands the test, not a hypothesis.

If we are thinking of God's work solely as it concerns God, we can call it experimental only in that vaguer sense which allows us to talk of experimental work in the arts. "Hunt's *Light of the World* strikes us as highly conventional. We forget that in its time it was an experimental picture." That is, Hunt was finding his way into a new style; he was not following a well-tried formula. In this sense God's work is experimental; not that he needs, like the artist, to find out what he can do by doing it; but that what he does is constantly new and, as we say, creative.

There is nothing the matter with such a line of thought, or with such a use of "experimental". Only it is beside the point of our present discussion. God does not need to prove general truths by particular tests, his worshippers do. They need to know that everything has God behind it; that God cares for the perfection of his creatures; that self-fulfilment lies in doing his will; and many similar principles of life or of existence. So what we want to say is that God's manipulation of his human material proves no principles to God, and so (in the scientific sense) is no experiment to him; but that it may have experimental value to us, and check for us our general beliefs.

"Well, but that is surely nonsense. The whole point about experiment in science is that it is something we arrange, control or manipulate. Watching the world go by is not experiment. If all we can do is to let God act, we shall never get beyond idle guesses of what he is at; and, as we agreed long ago, that isn't science. And in any case, we cannot even see God acting, let alone guess what he intends. All we can see is the world going by."

That would indeed be all, if all we could do were to let God act. But suppose we can do more – suppose he gives us a part to take in his actions. Then God's manipulations might become our experiments; and what forwarded his creative purposes might set us straight on the truths of religion.

To speak of God's "manipulations" is merely to force the parallel between the work of God and our experimental science. We manipulate the energies of nature, God does not. "Manipulation" is a forcible re-direction through external interference. God simply wills the energies of nature to act in their own way; that is why his doing what he does is invisible. All we see is what he does; and what he does is what, as willed by him, his creatures do. His lower creatures do what he wills, and never know it. How should they? They cannot so much as conceive the notion of God. Having in our capacity of reasonable thought some remote likeness to the mind which God is, we men can think of God; and so we may come not only to do his will, but to know that we do it.

Much of what we do in accordance with God's will is of no more experimental value to us in evidence of God than what we see other creatures do. I breathe, plants grow, water flows. All are natural processes and, as such, willed by God. And there is a great deal mixed in with my voluntary conduct which is equally natural, and no more than natural. I like what caresses my sense, and detest what jars upon it; I act to place myself in the way of the pleasure, and to take myself beyond reach of the annoyance.

But then there are active choices and choiceful acts of men which go beyond the fulfilment or gratification of their animal natures, and develop their personalities for good or for ill; which respect or dishonour, assist or hamper the personalities of others. Such acts must surely be seen to hasten or to delay, to further or to cross the creative purposes of God, if there is a God. For if there is, how can we doubt that he desires to make not merely human animals but noble souls, enriched with knowledge, active in kindness, strong in achievement? Men do not become so by bodily constitution alone; they become so by careful training, by strenuous effort, by generous action, both on their own part and on the part of others. If, then, it is the aim of God to make them what he would have them, it is an aim he will not in fact achieve except through what they do themselves by will and by choice. And when they act in this way it is possible for them to intend what God intends, and to intend it consciously. They may believe that they see the direction of his will, and they may fall in with it.

"What you say sounds very edifying, but I cannot see that it shows what you want it to show. You wish to claim that our doing of God's will has an experimental value in showing that there is a God and that he actually wills. But all it comes down to is that we guess God's will and act for ourselves in accordance with our guesses. I may say that I am doing the will of my great-aunt in Australia by keeping up a subscription in her name to the Putney dogs' home, but maybe I have no great aunt in Australia (she died last year) and maybe her last act was to call down the curse of heaven on the Putney dogs' home and all its inmates. You talk as though when we do someone's will, that person's will is a mysterious something which gets inside us and directs us, in the way in which our own will directs us; but that's nonsense, surely."

It is nonsense, yes, if we are talking great-aunts; but is it nonsense if we are talking theology? Great-aunts and great-nephews are outside one another, and so with all pairs of human persons. But how could God and his creatures be mutually external to one another in that way? Is not the whole hypothesis we are considering precisely this, that the will of God takes actual effect in what his creatures do of their own motion?

"I dare say; and so far as brutes or inanimate agents go, the hypothesis may pass – as a hypothesis. Such agents do not exercise deliberate choice; so let the deliberate choice behind their action be God's, if you like. But you are bound to make an exception of the human will. We do exercise deliberate choice, so how can the choice or the will be any-one's but our own? You have simply got to say that God abdicates his initiative so far as we are concerned and leaves decision to us. God's control over men's godly decisions must be like the control of advice over one who adopts it, not like the control of a writer's thought over his hand when he composes."

No, I am sorry, I can't agree. The exception which you are asking me to tack on to the hypothesis makes nonsense of the whole thing. It takes out of God's hands the action which is most characteristic of God and which in fact serves us as our specimen and clue for interpreting his action in general. In willing the physical world, we say God thinks physically and in thinking the animal world biologically. But he does not think physically because he is physical nor biologically because he is animal. He chooses to think physically because he chooses to make a physical world, and because he has the divine power to think what he makes exactly as it is to go. The act of thinking, even when it sets itself on physical lines, is itself as mental and as personal as all thinking is. Personality is the very nature of God's life; and where in the world does it obtain expression? Not in physical existence, not in animal existence, even ours; not in the part of our behaviour which is merely instinctive, but in our free, deliberate acts of mind. Since these are the very signature of God's authorship, how shall we deny them to be the work of his hand?

The point can be put with even greater force if we are allowed to go beyond the scope of our present argument, and to accept the Christian revelation. God is love. The conviction is Christian in origin, though it is accepted by multitudes of people who believe very few of the sentences in the Apostles' Creed. Now no thoughtful person, whether Christian or otherwise, supposes the love of God to consist of warm emotion or of animal instinct. His love is an endlessly generous choice, by which he actively fosters his creatures for their sakes and for what he sees in them. Very well; but we meet such love nowhere in the world but in our fellow-men; and what is more, nowhere but in their chosen and thoughtful acts or attitudes. If the highest, most voluntary part of human behaviour is not the act of God, then nowhere in the universe do we directly meet the divine love.

I will bring forward one more consideration from which the same point emerges. What is the most godlike thing God creates? Surely a person; and not just any sort of person, but a hero of charity, a saint. It is possible to wonder whether God would make any world at all, if it were going to bear no such fruits ever or anywhere. Now the godlike part of such a person does not lie in his bodily structure or even in his inherited aptitudes, but in what he does with these gifts of his own free will. Nothing but a life of noble decision and of well-directed action can build up that character of goodness which is the glory of God's handiwork. Only, of course, it is not God's handiwork, if our voluntary acts are not the acts of God at all. It is the man's handiwork. God set him going and put materials ready to his hand; the man made and executed the heavenly design; the supreme product of God's world is no creature of God after all, but of the human will. But whatever people may say in defence of an argument, in practice and in life no one with any belief in God believes that.

The relation of our godly action to God's action in us has never been found easy to think about; and if we made it look easy we might be sure that we were misrepresenting the facts. It would be absurd for us to attempt a full-dress staging of the discussion here. We will content ourselves with the point which belongs to our argument.

We have been looking at the suggestion that there is a simple contrast between the deliberate acts of men and all other sorts of activity the world contains. Physical or instinctive activity comes directly under the will of God; deliberate action does not. The comparison sounds straight enough, but what we have to say is, that it is by no means so straight as it sounds; in fact, it has been put all crooked. We will proceed to straighten it.

It is unreasonable to take as our subjects of comparison deliberate activity and physical activity. What we have to compare on the one side and on the other is the creature of God – his physical creature and his personal creature. Or rather, his sub-personal physical creature, and his personal physical creature; for persons are physical too; and the point is important. We are physical, *plus* . . . and of course it is the *plus* that specially interests us; but the physical must not be forgotten. Our bodies are made up of numberless units which just do what their structure prescribes in a blind, repetitive way. Their action is as automatic as the action of any physical elements anywhere.

Now if we want to compare the relation to God of men and of other things, it is man the thing, not man the person, who offers the obvious parallel; and we should start from there. For man the thing, in all his thingly parts and functions, must stand related to the divine will exactly as sub-human things are related. The cells in the tissue, the corpuscles in the blood, the living links in the nerve-chain all simply "do their stuff" as people vulgarly say, just as do the components in the bodies of the lowest animals, or indeed, of plants.

We can now put the difficulty of the comparison we are wrestling with somewhat more precisely. The difficulty is not, how on earth we should compare the expression of the divine will in physical activity with the expression of that will in deliberate activity. The difficulty is, to compare the divine will expressed in a creature who is just physical with the expression of that will in a creature who is physical *plus*. There seems to be a *plus* on the one side, and no *plus* on the other; and so we cannot see with what the *plus* should be compared.

What, then, are we to do? Suppose we glance back at our discussion of creation and of biological development. Were we content to say that the impress of the divine Will on the world consisted in causing physical systems or forces to keep blinding away in obedience to their own natures or constitutions – that it consisted in that and in nothing more? We were by no means content with such an account. We dwelt upon the astonishing way in which structure has built up, and systems have attained stability; how, without the simpler elements being forced or violated, or deprived of their proper action, they have been caught and held in new patterns. It appeared to us the masterpiece of God's creative skill, that forms should naturally and without violence arise out of forms which did not prefigure them.

So then there is after all a *plus* on the side of sub-human nature – a creative pull or persuasion of some kind leading to higher forms of existence. There is not only the will of God for things to keep fulfilling the nature they have; there is a further will for them to realise God's never-ceasing creative aims, through mazes of apparently chance change and random combination. And we remarked what is to human eyes the infinite patience of God in waiting on circumstance and opportunity, in allowing for setbacks and dead ends, so that the achievement of his further aims may be the natural work of forces and systems already established and active.

But now suppose a creature capable of looking beyond the mere maintenance of its existence-pattern, and able to feel or even understand the forward pressure of the divine will. Such a creature could surely ease and hasten the creative progress by acting in a line directly to serve its aims; for by so doing it could cut out age-long meanders of random experiment. It might care not only for its own best self but for all worthwhile existences which came its way; it might favour their self-realisation or their development; it might, according to its limited capacity, enter into the creative thoughts of God.

If there be such a creature, what are we to say of the relation between its intelligent choices and its Creator's will or choice? Is it less subject to his will than brute things or is it more so? It goes without saying that brute things have no power wilfully to resist the will of God, for they do nothing wilfully. They stand in the way of the swift or economical advance of the Creative Purpose by their sheer bruteness, and by the uncontrolled randomness of their collisions with others like them. We may not say that they defeat or delay the will of God itself, for God does not desire the impossible. He means the world to make itself from the bottom up, after its own fashion; and so his very purpose takes effect through all those apparently aimless blunderings on the part of nature which are the actual means to its achievement. The control of the Creative Purpose over the elements it steers is effective; and yet it is (humanly speaking) an enormously loose control.

Surely we must suppose that creative control over the intelligent creature we are imagining is closer, not looser; divine purpose not having to wait upon the action of brute agents which have no concern with it, but being served by one who has some notion of the part he should play in

God's larger designs. God will wait for him, too; but he will not wait so long. He will wait for delays and false starts due to limitations of view, downright errors, relapses, even, into brutal self-regard. But the grip of his purpose on the voluntary instrument will be firmer, because it offers more hold to him than brute things can do.

I hardly need to throw off so light a disguise as my story has put on, or to tell my readers what they have seen from the start. My imaginary creature is not imaginary at all; he is the human animal. For the purposes of making out my moral I have flattered our species, that is all. It is too much to claim for us that we are called to further God's aims in achieving new sorts of creatures. The best we can do is give existing species a chance, and let God employ us in the enrichment of our own; for man himself, even within humanity, is constantly going into a new creation.

That is by the way. Let us turn back to our parable, or comparison, or whatever we should call it, and extract the moral which concerns us. It is this. The will of God is in truth perfectly one, there is no rift or conflict anywhere in it. But we men in our attempts to think about it are bound to distinguish two strands in it, which God is, as it were, at pains to reconcile. There is his will for everything to be itself and act according to its kind, and there is his will for all things to work together towards further purposes. The first of these wills is, in a sense, basic, for everything must exist and be itself before it can serve any further purpose whatever. So the second will respects the first, and supplements it without violence to it, by a sort of persuasive pressure; and such is the divine will which takes effect through good men in their good actions.

Brute things are subject to the creative pressure, but being brute, cannot know they are. Enlightened men can not only coincide with its dictates, they can put themselves at its disposal. There is a union of wills in which God's will is inevitably directive and superior. Godly men know what they are doing; God's disposal of them becomes, through their association with its action, their experimental proof of religion. Let us paraphrase St. Thomas once more. "Experimental science concerns things we can work. But God is not to be worked by us. On the contrary, we men are his work", not only in our physical being, but more transparently in our moral existence. Nevertheless (we will now add) by associating our wills with his working of them, we acquire experimental acquaintance with the work of God.

The difference between experimental practice in religion on one hand and in natural science on the other is not arbitrary, unaccountable or surprising; it follows logically enough from the difference between the realities we are trying to know in each case, and from the different ways in which we are related to them. Physical things stand alongside us, and on a level with us – anyhow on a level with our bodies. They go about their business, we go about ours. We and they impinge on one another in the process, and that is how we become aware of them. If we wish to improve our acquaintance with them, we do it by systematic physical interference, seeing how they will react to conditions exactly defined by us and carefully set. That is physical experiment.

But God does not stand alongside us or on a level with us, nor do we become aware of him through any external collision, mutual impingement or interaction between his activity and ours. How could we? He is related to us in quite another way: as the will which underlies our existence, gives rise to our action and directs our aim. To look for God by the methods we use for examining nature would not be scientific, it would be silly. A microscope is a scientific instrument, but it is not scientific to look for a note of music through a microscope. How can we have experimental knowledge of the will behind our will? Only by opening our will to it, or sinking our will in it; there is no other conceivable way. We cannot touch God except by willing the will of God. Then his will takes effect in ours and we know it; not that we manipulate him, but that he possesses us.

The aim of natural science is not only to know. The experiments which confirm our general hypotheses also give us the confidence to manipulate natural forces for our practical advantage. It can happen that the crucial experiment which tests the hypothesis is a try-out of the very manipulation we wish to have at our command. To take a notorious example: the proof that atomic forces could be exploded was the success of an arranged explosion. But if the informative experiment may virtually be an anticipated practical application, the practical applications of the theory may serve also as informative experiments. They not only offer continuous confirmatory proof of the hypothesis on which they are based; they may also offer experimental evidence for extensions of theory. So between exploratory experiment and practical application there is no absolute barrier; the one can run into the other.

It is no great surprise, then, to observe that in religion the barrier vanishes; experiment and practical application are simply one. The only exploratory experiment available is the practical application. We cannot arrange set experiments on the divine will for a very plain reason; it would never be the divine will. There is only one divine will we can touch, and that is what God wills us to do here and now; and we can only find it by embracing it. And that is the same thing as to make a practical application, or use, of our relationship with God. For the "use" of the divine will to us (if such language is tolerable) is that it should act as the master, the guide and the inspiration of ours.

According to St. Matthew's story, Satan suggested to Jesus an arranged experiment on the divine will. Jesus was to jump from the temple cornice and see what the God of the temple would do. But since it was not the divine will that he should jump, his jumping would not be an experiment on the divine will – or only on that divine will which is the foundation of nature, and by which air is yielding and stones are hard. "Thou shalt not put the Lord thy God to the test," Christ quoted to Satan. Arranged experiments on the divine will are ruled out.

To bring the story closer to ourselves: if ever we pray to see whether prayer will work, it won't, because it won't be prayer anyhow. Prayer is a sincere seeking of the divine will; and if that is what we are doing, then that is what we are doing. We can experiment in the tranquillising or the uplifting effect of religious ceremonies, ritual recitations, pious make-believe, or reflection on Christian ideas. We can even experiment, if we think it worth trying, with the magical or telepathic effect of our prayer-spells on our neighbours. The probability of our deceiving ourselves over the results of such experiments is exceptionally high;

but we can do our best not to cheat. Only, however careful, our experiments will tell us nothing about God – no more, anyhow, than the sort of thing scientific experiments do tell us about God; that is, how some piece of nature has been made to run by him: the piece of nature in this case being the working of human psychology. If, on the contrary, we are to experience the sinking of our will in the divine will, then that is what we must be at – the sinking of it, by an obedient attention to his; and nowhere else can we have experience of God.

Several consequences follow from so drastic a limitation of the evidential field. One is that we cannot reason ourselves into faith by the experiment of union with God's will; for the experiment is no experiment unless it is an act of faith. We cannot perform the spiritual act of uniting our wills with the will of a God in whom we do not yet believe. The predicament of the would-be believer sounds awkward; but the awkwardness is mostly in the sound. It sounds awkward, "that we must already have faith before we can make the experiment on which our faith is to rest"; for if we already have the faith, the experiment is superfluous and if we have not the faith, we cannot make it. But people with a little experience of life know that dilemmas of this sort are made to be laughed at. "If the girl and I do not love one another, we cannot approach one another on the affectionate footing which will let us discover whether we love one another or not." Who is going to be frightened by this sort of difficulty? It can be taken for granted that stirrings of love are already present; were they not, no question would arise whether or not the thing would be a match. Besides, an inclination towards the other sex is natural; it is not like "My only opportunity to learn tennis is to join the club, but I really can't join the club until I've learnt tennis". Tennis does not come by nature, liking does, and so does faith; in those at least who have come near enough to it to be concerned about it. The practical difficulty is that faith shares our hearts with so many other attitudes, that though it is somewhere there, it does not prevail. But as we allow our faith to act, it obtains mastery; by the experiment of faith we advance from faith to faith; we obtain assurance, "the proof of things invisible".

Another consequence of what we have said is that the experimental evidence of God lies in the possession of our will by his and in nothing else. If an action and a will proceeding from the divine centre, and not simply from our centre, is not convincing, nothing experimental will be so; if we are not assured that the integration of our will into the divine puts us where we belong, that the God who undertakes us is nothing less than God, then no experimental evidence is going to convince us.

We can fairly look for accompanying signs, but they are not decisive. By signs I mean happy effects. It is natural to expect that the integration of our will with the Creative Will should enhance, enrich and bless our personal being, and others through us. On the supposition that God is truly what we believe him, it would be odd if our giving ourselves to him made us on the whole more restless, more frustrated, less able to manage our relations with others or to discipline our own passions, less generous or outgoing, less alive all over. The signs of blessing can fairly be looked for; but at the best they are confirmatory evidence of a relationship which must be its own proof. No one can say that wherever such enrichments of life are present, there is bound to be an active dependence on the divine will. We may go farther; there may be a heroic service of God and no such blessed signs be visible at all. For sometimes the will of God which his servants must embrace is not aimed at their present or personal advantage; it pursues a more distant creative purpose. The individual's service may be a martyrdom, with no fruits in this world but agony and personal destruction. So Christ was crucified.

A third consequence, and the last we will mention here, is that an experimental relation to God requires no apparatus, no set moves or technique of method. For it lies in a relation of will to will; and such a relation can be achieved at any time, by thinking, deciding, acting. If a man is in a position really to think of God's will, and heartily to embrace it, there is nothing more he need do; let him get on with it. Only this "really to think and heartily to embrace" is no small matter. With most of us it takes more than a simple movement of the mind to recall that God is God, and to appreciate either the generosity which is the substance of his will, or the particular concern which is the direction of it. It takes some doing, so to gather ourselves together in face of these realities, that we can greatly care or firmly resolve. There are many useful techniques and customary practices for putting ourselves in a state to embrace God's will. And so people write books of spiritual method; they sound scientific and they are in fact based on much experience. But let us be clear that if there is science here it is science about the human soul, and how to prepare it; not science about God, or how our will can be his. There is no technique for that; God's will is simply to be willed.

7

THE ONENESS OF RELIGION

I hope no one who has troubled to read so far will have mistaken my intention. I am not pretending to give a balanced or all-round view of religion. I am exhibiting the sort of parallel to scientific activity which religion offers. That is, I am taking religion as an exploration of realities, the realities in this case being divine. Such a way of viewing religion is perfectly legitimate; it is never perhaps central and for some minds not even necessary. How many good souls have walked humbly with their God and never seen him as an object of exploration at all? Only, once we have called the truth of religion in question, we begin to grope for the realities it purports to describe, and until we feel we have encountered solid fact, cannot well get on with the practice of our faith.

So, then, what I have said about religious action as experimental evidence is a very limited account of the spiritual life. Even so, I should be sorry if it seemed not merely limited in scope, but negative or cramping in tendency. If someone else had written this book and I were reading it, that is the way I think I should judge it. "This man," I should complain, "confines the experimental evidence of religion to such a pin-point area as to make it virtually invisible. It is to be something entirely inward, the touch of one's will with the divine will. And not content with confining the fact to the believer's heart, he rules most of the heart out too. The evidence is not to lie in one's general state of feeling, in any poetry of imagination or rapture of joy, in any guidance of wisdom or strength of virtue, but solely in the fine point where will is rooted in will." So I think I should complain, were the book anyone else's; for we are all severe critics of other men's work while judging our own, of course, with limitless indulgence. In fact I am writing this book, and so I am convinced that nothing I have said justifies the criticism I have imagined; I am sure I have a power of sensible argument up my sleeve ready to rush out and sweep away the objection, should anyone be so perverse as to advance it.

I cannot ask my readers to be as indulgent to me as I am to myself. Still, I will ask them to float me a little benevolence, as it were on short-term loan, to see whether in these few remaining pages I can clear my credit.

I shall begin by simply denying that I have shut the evidence within the heart at all. A man's embracing of the divine will is, of course, a personal act on his part; and you can say if you like that all a man's personal acts spring from his heart; for that is no more than a poetical way of saying that they are his personal acts and no mere automatic performances. They come from the heart – he means them; and certainly it is from his heart, not anyone else's, that they must come. But they are not locked inside his heart. A man can speak to his friends from the heart, and from the heart do them services. The acts by which the will of God is embraced similarly employ the hands and the tongue. It was not only by his prayer in Gethsemane that Jesus embraced the will of God; it was by stopping the brawl at his arrest and by surrendering himself; it was by maintaining his royal claim before the High Priest and the Roman Governor; by refusing the doped wine, by praying for his executioners, and by all his acts and words on that memorable day. Ideally speaking, the embracing of God's will has the whole of a man's conduct for its outward expression. However far the common Christian may be from such a state of sanctity, he is at least aware that there is nothing of importance he does which cannot in principle express his obedience.

But if a man's embracings of the divine will are not shut within his heart, still less so is the divine will which he embraces. We are not to think of God's will as a shy secret hidden somewhere under the root of our mind, and there to be dived for. God's will is written across the face of the world. What else have we been looking at in our discussions? The God of religion is not different from the God of rational inquiry. To see into the active cause of the world is to find a sovereign and creative will; and that is the will which religion embraces. Not indeed that the pious Christian is called upon to become God's instrument in shaping the heavens, or in the evolution of species still unborn and unthought. The divine will touches us in that detail of the whole design which involves us. But even this fragment of the universal purpose is not buried in the soil of our minds, to be groped for by our inward musings. It is projected on our practical environment. God's will is my neighbour's good, and to see it I must look at my neighbour. What is God sustaining, what is he making or perfecting in that person? And what does his work there demand on my part? If Dives wants to find the will of God, let him look at Lazarus. How much longer are his sores to go untended or his hunger unfed?

The case of Lazarus at the rich man's door speaks for itself. A man miserably ill and hopelessly poor calls to the most insensitive conscience, and even, one might say, to animal feeling. Yet, says Christ's parable, the man of wealth may pass poor Lazarus by. What can be done for hearts to which such misery does not speak? Christ says, "Let them heed Moses and the Prophets", the teachings, that is, of their people's religion. So "Moses and the Prophets" may be needed to bring the plainest of duties home to the heart. But what of duties which are not plain at all, when we do not readily see for ourselves which way the will of God draws us, or what is the creative purpose of which we are the instruments? Then Moses and the Prophets, then Christ and the Saints, by opening our eyes to the grand lines of God's design, will bring the case of our neighbour into a truer perspective.

The will of God, then, is not a secret to be dug from the ground of the heart; it is chiefly displayed in the demands of our environment. Neither is the will with which we embrace that will a treasure locked in the heart; its function is to be the soul of our conduct. Only the touch of God's will on ours is utterly personal to us, and how could it be otherwise? Yet even the treasure of the heart is shared by communication. What can be more inward, more personal than a deep and genuine sexual devotion? And yet it is folly to deny that it can be communicated. Lovers have written their love in prose and in verse, and there is no writing that speaks to us more directly; for we are the same sort of creatures as they are. If we had no inclination to love, or had never found anyone lovable, we should not understand them. But as it is, they not only move our sympathy, they shape our attitudes and fashion our affections. Sexual passion is native to the human animal, but romantic devotion is the fruit of cultivation. It is a tradition slowly built up, of which the growth and the history can be read in the art of ages. The poets have taught us to love with depth and with refinement. And yet no one who has a heart will say that romantic love is a freak of fashion, an etiquette of courtship we might as well have done without; so convinced we are that it opens our eyes to real qualities in what we love, and to possibilities of relationship most highly to be prized.

The comparison with religion is obvious. Our souls are as truly made for God as our hearts for one another; but religion, like romantic love, is a long tradition of spiritual cultivation. Moses and the Prophets, Christ and the Saints have built up attitudes and formulations which are or should be second nature to modern Christians. They have given us eyes, and because we see with them, we laugh at those who tell us that an eyeless state is more realistic. They have opened possibilities to us of such privilege that we cannot be persuaded to pass them by.

Yet the parallel of romantic love gives but a faint idea of the part played by others' testimony in our religion. Poets and novelists have taught us to love; yet however instructive the examples they never exactly apply. Our Joan is not Dante's Beatrice. Besides, once we have settled down to Joan we go on with her. There she is, a piece of flesh and blood; her ways draw our affection and her wishes direct our service. In religion it is not like this. I do not look to meet with another God, something like the God of St. Paul or St. Augustine, but still a God all my own; for God is one. And when, directed by St. Augustine or St. Paul, I enter into some beginnings of relation with this God, I do not immediately become independent of their testimony. For God is not simply there, so that I have merely to go on with him, as we go on with those we have begun to love, taking our cue from their words, their behaviour, and the look in their eyes. God is indeed there, for he is everywhere and in all things; but his person is hidden in his works and exalted above our conceiving. He is personally disclosed in the human acts and thoughts which he personally inspires; but then the disclosure is full in proportion as the response is holy and the inspiration deep. I should be a fool indeed if I took my godly actions and thoughts (supposing I have any which deserve the epithet) as providing a disclosure of God equal to the disclosure he made in the lives and the minds of heroic saints. If I had not the least experience of what it is to apply my will to God's, I should not understand what St. Paul or St. Augustine was talking about. Once allowing that the slender clue is in my hands, I may hope to learn more about God from them than I can from my own life. I will be happy if I can look through their eyes.

In some such way a trifler in verse may be helped by his doggerel efforts to see what verse-writing is, and to understand the finer points of true poets; and the humdrum student of physics may be helped by his own nibbles at research to appreciate the inventive genius of Newton or of Einstein. Only it is to be noted that if he does so, he will not be studying science, he will be studying creative genius. While that is his aim, he will be in some sort of parallel with the student of religion; for he, too, is studying creative power – though a creative power centred in God, rather than in his human instruments. The study of inventive genius in his predecessors is not, of course, the scientist's proper business. Getting inside Newton's head is an exploration of scientific ability, not an exploration of scientific fact. The scientist does not depend on his predecessors as a Christian may on St. Paul or St. John, to see the truth through their eyes. He depends on them, because they have done a lot of work for him, and it would be folly not to go on from where they left off. He cannot repeat all their experiments or rework every item of their calculations, for he has not the time. But in principle the thing could be done. It may have required genius to devise experiments; it requires only routine competence to repeat them; and so too with the thinking through of theories. A theoretical astrophysicist who has completed his studies and still cannot appreciate Einstein's reasoning is not merely no Einstein, he is a fool at physics.

So the scientist may be endlessly indebted to his predecessors and full of admiration for the great pioneers, but he is not dependent upon their authority; he need not trust them an inch, for he can always check their arguments or repeat their experiments. It cannot be like this in religion, and that for a very simple reason – the experiments cannot be repeated. As we have said, the sole experiment possible in that field is the embracing of God's will. But the will of God is a particular will for every man in every situation; and what God gives the humdrum Christian to do would not so fully reveal God, even were it perfectly performed, as the task he lays upon the heroic saint. "Even if he did it perfectly." And he will not. The sensitivity and the virtue required to do God's will in a way that might make it deeply revealing is not a standard of competence to be taken for granted in the common practitioner, like the standard of competence we can safely expect of trained scientific researchers. And so there are two reasons why spiritual experiments cannot be repeated. The experimental event cannot be reproduced, and the experimental ability cannot be guaranteed.

So the experiments of religion cannot be repeated. But what about the theories? St. Paul and St. John and St. Augustine not only experienced God's will, they thought about God and gave their thoughts to us. Even if we must trust them for the experiments, need we trust them for the theories? Must we swallow their theology? Cannot we check their arguments and reconstruct their formulations?

It would be absurd not to raise the question – indeed, it arises of itself. But it would take a book to answer it; and then the answer would not be a plain Yes or No. Yes, for of course the most conservative of us do and must rethink the theology of the saints if we are to use it or live by it. We are bound to rid St. Paul's pages of elements which we can only regard as First-Century period junk. Nor is that all: the Christian conscience has acquired certain sensitivities to which the First Century was a stranger. We are not going to feel with St. Paul about the sovereignty of husbands over wives or about the ethics of punishment.

So much for the Yes. Now for a few words on the No. We cannot agree that the religious thought of the saints is as separable from their experience of God as theories are from experiments in science. We cannot simply say, "Hold fast to the experimental facts, but freely rethink the theories based upon them." For in physical science the experimental data are physical, recorded in most cases by physical instruments. If the instruments have been correctly read and the readings correctly recorded, we have the facts independently of any theoretical constructions. Perhaps it is not proper to talk about experimental data in spiritual experience at all; but if we can talk of them they are certainly nothing like this. The willing of God's will in us happens in our mind and through our mind, so how can it be independent of the way we think? St. Paul could not have experienced God's will in the way he did, if he had neither absorbed the Old Testament nor recognised in Christ the fulfilment of Old Testament promises.

Since I am not going to launch into a whole book on the question which has dropped into my lap, I must be content with a lame answer. We must rethink the thought of our masters in faith radically enough to make it genuinely ours. We must not and we cannot strip their testimony down to bare facts and reconstruct on our own account the "theories" which in their minds supported the facts. For the "theories" were not theories about the experience; they were the vital form of the experience itself.

It is easy to illustrate the point from a human example. You cannot separate the bare facts of a friendship from what the friends think of one another. Yet however genuine the friendship, and however manifestly based in realities rather than illusions, you cannot adopt their whole way of regarding one another as your estimate of the persons involved. You will do much rethinking, to arrive at your own estimate. But that will not necessarily mean that you have separate sources of information about these people, apart from what they tell you of one another or of themselves. Suppose you know nothing about them except from their letters, which you come across in an old chest, tied up with faded tape. You will not claim on such evidence to know them better than they knew themselves, or knew one another. And yet you will be bound to think your own thoughts about them, not theirs.

I have been trying to write in this book about the approach to religious belief from the side of science. I have been concerned with the doctrine of God, and his creation of the natural world; and I have come so far as to say something about that direct experience of God's creative will, which alone gives reality or practical point to our pondering over the cause of the universe. It has not been my purpose to write about faith in Jesus Christ, for that is surely a different side of the matter. All the same, I should be sorry to lay down my pen without any attempt to relate the doctrine of God I have sketched with the doctrine of the Saving Incarnation.

I suppose it is a fairly common opinion that the suggestions offered to our minds by a contemplation of the natural world on the one hand, and by the message of the Gospel on the other, are strikingly different. Nature suggests to us a hidden universal power, sustaining an infinity of created beings or forces in existence, and exercising on their natural motions a widely spread and infinitely patient creative influence or persuasion. The Gospel presents to us a God of history, concerned to gather mankind under the kingship of his will by first educating one tribe of men into the knowledge of himself; a God so personal, so particular and so present, that he collects his whole purpose for the world into one speaking action, by the entry of the divine life into the created sphere in the body and person of a man. Unlike the God of nature, who shapes wayward elements with endless patience and is content with such higher creative achievements as the natural action of natural agents allows, the God of the Gospel has fixed a day; he has uttered a challenge of love and of wrath, which men must accept or reject, once and for all determining their destinies. And no longer content to get his harvest from the slow ripening of the world he has made, he sweeps it aside and fashions anew beyond the curtain of death a world of deathless perfection.

It is possible to see this sharp contrast between the God of Nature and the God of Gospel and yet to believe that they are the same God. However surprising the Gospel may be to the student of nature, he may be convinced by it and willing to accept it. He may tell himself that Nature speaks anyhow with an uncertain voice, and that it is mere intellectual conceit on our part to trust the ideas of God which we may frame for ourselves on such baffling evidence. Until the lightening bursts from the cloud and the divine appears in man we have no right to any opinion beyond a reverent agnosticism. With the message of the Gospel in our heart, we may turn back to the world of nature, and look for the hand of the Father of Jesus where his Spirit enables us to trace it.

Such is the attitude which many people knowingly or unknowingly adopt; and it is an attitude which allows them to get on with being Christians. But it is not the attitude I would recommend to anyone who can do better; otherwise I would scarcely be bothering to write this book. It is an attitude which involves an element of mental strain and intellectual violence; it agrees badly with the serenity of a true faith.

What I shall say by way of reconciliation will be nothing new; I shall draw out principles already laid down. We have said that the God to whom nature points is a Creator who thinks physical things physically, and all other things similarly as they are and as they act. But though such a power may think physical thoughts about the physical, it cannot itself be physical, for physical things as such do not think. The physical world reveals some part of what God thinks, it cannot reveal what he is. It is only when God makes a thinking creature that his work reveals part of what he is as well as part of what he thinks.

In fact the thinking creature, man, reveals God in two different ways. He serves as a sketch and he serves as a pencil. He serves as a sketch by simply being personally what he is – a thinker, a chooser, a maker and a lover. For it is on the model of these characteristics or activities that we form whatever conception of deity we ever do form. He serves as a pencil, by putting into the hand of God an instrument with which God can directly express his purpose, his character and his thought. Every decent man above the utterly primitive serves as a sketch or model for the mere notion of God. He has the powers which make a person, and though he has his limitations and shortcomings, not to mention malice or wickedness, we can readily think them away when we form the idea of deity. But to act as a pencil in God's hand is not given to a man in virtue of his mere humanity. No doubt the possibility is in some sense always there, but to realise the actuality is another matter.

This is not the place to launch into a treatise on the rebels against divine sovereignty which usurp the heart of man; and if we wrote the treatise it might add nothing to the reader's own acquaintance with the world, the flesh and the devil. Knowing ourselves, we are not surprised to find that the record of revelation is a history of the struggles of the human will against the mastery of God; or to be told that it was after long preparation, in one place and in one person, that complete mastery was achieved and a complete identification manifested of the human with the divine.

What have we said? Merely that the idea of a God of nature has two parts: his thoughts are physical; he is himself a thinker. And of these two parts the first cannot stand up without the second; God cannot be even guessed at, and never was guessed at, from nature alone, but only and always with the aid of the human model. Once this has been grasped, there is no special difficulty in thinking together the theology of nature and the faith of God incarnate as man; no difficulty in perceiving what St. John meant, when he said that what put on flesh and blood in Jesus was the thought or creative utterance which made the world.

We have not yet finished our task; but the same principle will see us through. The God of nature, we said, is infinitely patient; he is content to realise over millions of years the creative possibilities which lie in the natural action of created forces. Not so, it seems, the God of Gospel. He gives us a few years in which to make a once-for-all decision; and he is so little content with the possibilities allowed him by the created world, that he sets it aside and creates spiritual perfection for redeemed mankind on the other shore of death.

The contrast is undeniable; but it does not express different conceptions of God; it expresses the different actions of one God whose character it is to act appropriately in every field of his activity. The reasoning person is alone the off-print of God's nature and so alone deemed worthy of fellowship with him or of everlasting perfection. The work of creation makes the species but the work of salvation redeems the individual. Persons are called upon to make a once-for-all decision, since they are capable of it. When mind and will can be appealed to, why wait for the slow exploitation of blundering accident?

I have now finished what I have meant to say and I will say no more. But in taking leave I will reflect a moment on what I have done, or tried to do. I have stated as well as I could a theology of nature. I have stated the bare bones of the matter; I have tried to keep to what is essential and ought to be agreed. I have said nothing which is exciting, original or ingenious; because such suggestions, however exhilarating or intriguing, lead into uncertainties and are no basis for faith.

I have tried to write plainly. I know very well that everything I have written can be pulled to pieces by subtle philosophers; but then I think I also know that it can be put together again by philosophers no less subtle. The philosophical tug-of-war can be taken for granted. In the process of it the statement of the issue gets somewhat clarified; but belief is seldom settled by it one way or the other. There is a grid of hard thinking which gives shape and solidity to theistic belief, and which cannot be thrown over by Christians without self-stultification. It is this grid that I have made it my aim to put together in my discussions.

This is how it goes, and how it will in essentials continue to go when the philosophers have done with it. It is what the philosophers ought to examine, if they want to examine the theology of Nature. It is true and forcible in itself, and not because they give it (if they do give it) their approval.

But I do not want to talk so much about critical philosophers as about superior-minded theologians. The plain grid of hard thinking does not please them because, they say, the God of Nature is infinitely mysterious, and to argue about him in this hard and definite way is either presumptuous on our part or simply childish. But to talk like this is to saw off the branch on which one sits. It is the plain grid of hard thinking which alone gives us any notion of a God of Nature – even a God of Nature to be agnostic about. You want to realise the mysterious immensity of God. And how will you set about it? By sitting with your head in your hands, and your mind in a perfect fog, while you ask yourself what, if anything, you have a right to affirm? It will not get you far. Suppose on the contrary you think as clearly as you can in ordinary words of which you know the meaning, and set before yourself the Creative Mind which sees all things as they are in their true natures, willing them to be themselves and, through an infinity of chance combinations, leading them into the realisation of higher forms – what will your reaction be to such a subject of contemplation? Are you in any great danger of exclaiming, "Just so, I see the trick of it! I've got the formula! I'd only need to kick off this body, and equip myself with direct spiritual power, and I'd run the world for you! I'd weave the Universe!" The infinite majesty of God can take care of itself. The harder and more clearly we think out the thoughts which give rise to the very idea of God, the more we shall be overwhelmed with the mystery which confronts us.

God is at once infinitely remote from us and perfectly familiar to us. He is remote by what he is, he is familiar in what he does, for he identifies his thought with the thing he makes and moulds his care for it on its existence. So the mind of God becomes all things and is directly presented by what anything truly is. "He is not far from any one of us, for by him we live and move and have our being" not only as souls or persons, but as animals and even as parcels of physical stuff. His will is in the drawing of our breath and in the pulses of our heart; how much more in the movement of our affection or the aspiration of our hope! Above all, he takes the form of our action when he inspires us, when we let our will be the instrument of his. To realise a union with our Creator we need not scale heaven or strip the veil from ultimate mystery; for God descends into his creature and acts humanly in mankind. He has made it our calling that we should have fellowship with himself; and so now by faith, but in heaven by sight, we are to look into the countenance divinely human and humanly divine of Christ the Lord.

Austin Farrer was a Fellow of the British Academy and Warden of Keble College, Oxford until his death in 1968. A preacher of profundity and wit, he was also a renowned philosopher and theologian. There have been few better advocates for universal, deep-rooted, mature Christianity.